Wood Finishing and Refinishing

Wood Finishing and Refinishing

BY THE EDITORS OF

CREATIVE HOMEOWNER PRESS

CREATIVE HOMEOWNER PRESS®

A DIVISION OF FEDERAL MARKETING CORPORATION, 24 PARK WAY, UPPER SADDLE RIVER, NEW JERSEY 07458

Manufactured in United States of America

Current Printing (last digit)
10 9 8 7 6 5 4

Executive Editor: Shirley M. Horowitz
Editor: Marilyn M. Auer
Art Director: Léone Lewensohn
Designers: Léone Lewensohn, Paul Sochacki
Additional Illustrations: Norman Nuding

Cover photo provided by S&S Construction
Co., Shapell Industries, Inc., 8383 Wilshire Bou-
levard, Beverly Hills, CA 90211

We wish to extend our thanks to Mr. J.T. Benson, Mr. Donald Mortensen, and Mr. Gordon
Phillips of S.C. Johnson & Son, Inc. and Mr.
Carl Bullmore of Architectural Woodworking
Co. for their suggestions and technical review
of the manuscript, and to Mr. Robert Larson
of Vikwood Ltd. for his information on fine
wood veneers. The names and addresses of
all those who contributed to this volume can
be found at the back of the book. The page
number appears on page 7.

ISBN: 0-932944-54-X (paperback)
ISBN: 0-932944-53-1 (hardcover)
LC: 81-69641

CREATIVE HOMEOWNER PRESS®
BOOK SERIES

A DIVISION OF FEDERAL
MARKETING CORPORATION
24 PARK WAY,
UPPER SADDLE RIVER, NJ 07458

Projects

Contents

Wood is an enduring, useful and beautiful material. When worn, the finish that protects the surface can be restored and the wood preserved.

1

All About Wood

This is a book about wood, new and old, throughout your home. Whatever the condition of the wood, you undoubtedly want it to look its best. When you build a piece of furniture, or some other project, from scratch, you may select any material you want (assuming that the desired material is available) and finish the project any way you wish—within the restrictions of your time and budget. If you are refinishing paneling, woodwork, floors or a piece of furniture, however, your choices are limited by the existing wood and the existing finish. The existing finish will dictate what must be used to remove it. The existing wood will dictate what you must do to create the final finish you want. Therefore, it is a good practice to understand wood, its peculiar and particular characteristics, so you will be able to select and to apply the proper finish.

CHARACTERISTICS OF WOOD

Wood can generally be divided into two categories: softwood and hardwood. These designations, however, do not indicate the relative hardness of the material; they refer to the kind of tree from which the wood comes. Trees that are coniferous (cone-bearing), such as pine, are called softwoods. Trees that shed their leaves are deciduous and are considered hardwoods, regardless of the actual hardness of the wood. While most commercially made furniture is of hardwood, one softwood, pine, also is a popular wood for furniture.

Whatever the wood involved in your project, there are several significant properties of the wood that will influence the final appearance of the finished product: type of grain, durability, hard-

The natural color of wood may be enriched or altered with stains, paint and clear finishes. Here, new and old wood with different finishes are combined to create an attractive kitchen.

ness, workability with tools, color and overall appearance.

The Effects of Grain

One of the obvious characteristics of wood is grain. Although most people respond to the appearance of the grain, for the wood finisher, the primary concern is whether the grain is open or closed. Some wood grain looks fine but has large pores; this creates an open grain. Small pores in a wood create a closed grain.

Using Open-Grained Wood In furniture making, four of the most commonly used open-grained woods are walnut, oak, African or Honduras mahogany.

To create the smooth, even surface usually desired in a furniture finish, open-grained wood is commonly filled before finishing. A soft filler material is rubbed on and into the wood to fill the pores. If the filler is not used, the finish applied will seep into the open pore areas in greater quantities than will soak

The appearance of wood grain significantly affects the impression made by furniture. The swirling pattern shown here is called burl.

The grain of the mahogany in this antique secretary is part of the overall design. The color and grain emphasize the lines of the piece.

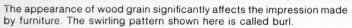

This old table is made of maple. The grain of the wood has been carefully matched on the top of the table and shows in the gatelegs.

GRAIN CHARACTERISTICS

Wood	Hardwood	Softwood	Open Grain	Close Grain
Ash	X		X	
Basswood	X			X
Beech	X		X	
Birch	X			X
Boxwood	X			X
Butternut	X		X	
Cedar		X		X
Cherry	X			X
Chestnut	X		X	
Cypress		X		X
Ebony	X			X
Elm	X		X	
Fir		X		X
Gum (Eucalyptus)		X		X
Hickory	X		X	
Holly	X			X
Mahogany	X		X	
Maple	X			X
Oak	X		X	
Pear	X			X
Pine		X		X
Redwood		X		X

into the closed areas. This will create an unsightly, rippled effect. The unfilled surface also will be rough; filler makes the surface smooth and even.

Using Closed-Grained Wood The popular furniture woods that are closed-grained are birch, maple, pine, fir, beech, gum and poplar. These woods usually are not filled or are filled with only a very thin filler. Examples of close-grained wood with very tiny pores are basswood and holly. Basswood is seldom used for furniture, but holly is sometimes used in cabinets.

Grain Appearance Wood gets its grain pattern from the way the tree grows and from the way the logs are sawed. The grain, of course, contributes to the appearance of the final boards. The grain can be delicate and dense, as in maples, or bold and prominent like fir, or more moderate as in oak.

When the grain lines in wood are wide, widely separated and very noticeable, the grain is said to be coarse. If the lines are thin, delicate and close together, the wood is described as fine grained. If the lines of the grain are various distances apart, then the grain is called uneven. Regularly spaced grain lines are designated as even grain. Grain that is parallel to the axis of a log is straight grain. If, however, the wood layers go around the axis, they create spiral grain.

Grain and Sawing The appearance of the grain also is affected by the way the wood is cut. The two common methods are quarter sawed and plain sawed.

Quarter Sawing Quarter-sawed boards are cut perpendicular to the growth rings. The log is cut into quarters, lengthwise, and then each quarter is sliced into boards. The boards are cut at a 45-degree angle to the flat sides of the quartered log. Because of the direction of the cuts, the boards all have radial grain. This is less likely to warp and is generally considered to create a very strong board. However, many very narrow boards are created when the wood is cut this way. Most of these narrow boards are too small to be of use.

Riff Sawing Riff sawing is similar to quarter sawing except that long and short boards are cut alternately from the log. The angle of the cuts vary slightly from one board to another and small wedges of wood are wasted between the boards. However, this wastage is less than in quarter sawing.

Either of these cuts produces a strong, physically attractive board. The inherent waste does add significantly to the cost.

Plain Sawing To get the most boards with the least waste from a log, the standard way of cutting lumber is plain sawing. When a log is plain sawed, it is cut straight through from one side to the other. This creates relatively narrow board from two sides, but most of the boards are wide enough to be ripped into narrower, standard boards.

If you have a choice because you are building a piece from scratch, it would be advisable to use straight-grained woods for parts that provide structural support such as legs and arms. Straight grain gives more strength than cross grain. If you have a choice between quarter-sawed and plain-sawed wood, select the quarter-sawed material. It is less likely to warp and, therefore, to ruin your project.

Acceptance of Finishes
Some woods naturally are more able to

Application of a stain can change the entire character of a piece of wood, giving it a new color and making the grain pattern apparent.

accept certain kinds of finishes than others. Close-grained woods, for example, accept stains better than coarse, open-grained woods. However, with the use of fillers, sealers and other materials, careful preparation and use of final finishing methods detailed in this book, the natural acceptance abilities of the wood become academic. You can do just about anything you wish to wood. You can take a relatively inexpensive wood like pine and, with correct application of the proper stain, make it look like a piece of walnut. However, relatively inexpensive is truly a relative term/ costs of wood keep rising all the time.

Durability
Another characteristic of wood you will want to consider, assuming that you are either building a piece for scratch or making major repairs to an existing piece, is durability. This quality is dependent upon the hardness of the wood. The harder the wood, the better it will resist wear, scratches and dents. There

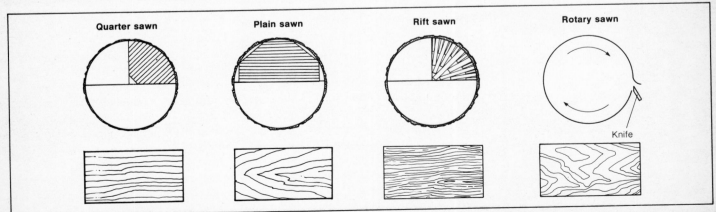

Quarter sawn   Plain sawn   Rift sawn   Rotary sawn

Knife

The appearance of the grain and the relative strength of boards is determined by the wood itself and the way in which the boards are sawn.

DURABLE HARDWOODS

Wood	Characteristics
Ash	Wears well
Beech	Resists abrasion
Cherry	Hard to dent, difficult to work
Chestnut	Easy to work, limited availability
Ebony	Hard to work, limited availability, expensive
Hickory	Very hard, difficult to work, subject to decay and insect infestation
Maple	Resists abrasion
Oak	Hard to dent
Walnut	Hard to dent

This solid wood countertop is of maple, a very hard wood. The surface has been protected and made waterproof by the application of seven coats of marine spar varnish.

Oak is a frequent choice for woodwork and kitchen cabinets because it is attractive, strong, and will withstand prolonged, heavy use.

are some exceptions, as noted in our chart. The hardness of the wood is a very important consideration in furniture. Unless you are building something that will sit in an out-of-the-way place or receive little use, you will want to build your project of durable wood.

This highboy is made of walnut, maple and pine. The hardwoods used are very durable and strong. Pine is softer and easily dented.

Workability of Wood

Wood may also be considered in terms of how easy it is to work with tools. That is, how it can be cut and shaped and how it holds fasteners.

The workability of wood varies to some degree, but if you use power tools with appropriate and sharp bits and blades and follow standard construction procedures, the workability of the wood you are considering for a project should not be too great a factor in your choice. If you are working exclusively with hand tools and you have trouble maintaining a sharp edge on these tools, you will want to work with softer woods. These softer woods, of course, will dent and mar more easily. Remember, too, that wood may split if nails or screws are driven in too near the ends of the board.

Judging the Appearance

Two important factors in the choice and finishing of wood are the color and over-all appearance. You should also consider the grain pattern and the probability of matching grain. If you are going to paint the wood, you do not have to be concerned about the appearance of the grain. You will, however, need to be concerned with sealing the surface so

that the grain will not rise when you apply the wet paint. Your final decision will have to be based on a selection of woods available at your lumber dealer. Your final choice should be of a wood that is the best compromise between the visual and physical requirements and the cost.

BUYING WOOD
Sizes of Furniture Grade Planks

Unlike construction grade wood that is cut to size and then allowed to dry and shrink below it nominal size, fine woods meant for furniture or cabinetmaking are cut larger than nominal size. This is true of all hardwoods and of furniture grade softwoods such as pine.

The furniture grade wood is kiln- or air-dried after sawing. The drying process reduces the bulk of the wood by approximately 10 percent. The boards are then sold in designations called "quarter stock."

If you need a board that is one inch thick, order a board that is 5/4. This is a board that is cut to one and one-quarter inches thick, dried and finish dressed to one and one-sixteenth inch thick. If necessary, you can plane down the difference.

Local Access

It should be noted that you probably will not have access to all of the types of wood discussed below. Many are in limited supply and available only on special order or from suppliers that specialize in furniture quality stock. Normally, a lumberyard stocks wood that is indigenous to the immediate area. One or another type of pine is usually plentiful, and you may find that a yard will stock at least one form of mahogany. Because of the increased costs, dealers will not handle wood that has to be shipped a great distance. If you are willing to accept shipping costs as a part of the price, you usually will be able to special order any wood you want. However, you will have to accept the boards that arrive as is, even if they are not exactly what you had envisioned.

Types of Woods

Ash Ash is an extremely hard hardwood. Because it is so hard, the wood is usually used for baseball bats and tool handles. It is a creamy white color with very little grain pattern. It is, however, open grained and must be filled before finishing. Although strong, it can be worked quite easily. It also is remarkably flexible; you can bend it more than other woods without the danger of its splitting.

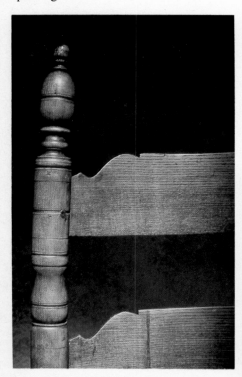

This ladderback chair is made of maple and ash, two very strong woods. Ash is also remarkably flexible and will bend under pressure.

Basswood This is a white wood that normally has very little grain showing. It is a light, easy-to-work wood. It is not as hard as some other hardwoods but is close grained. Basswood normally is used in making the interior parts of cabinets and as a core material, or banding, for plywood. It is not normally used as a finish material—i.e., exposed to view; but when used, it takes a good finish.

Birch This attractive hardwood is normally yellow/white to red. The com-mercially cut wood is yellow birch. It is close pored and does not need to be filled. A strong wood, it is still fairly easy to work. However, it is expensive, often more expensive than mahogany.

Cedar (Western Red) This wood is used mostly outside the house for shingles and small structures, such as storage buildings, because it has a very high resistance to weather and rot. It ranges in color from pink brown to plain brown and is easy to work and finish. Some people use cedar shingles inside the house as a decorative element on one or more of the walls. No filler is required for the wood.

Cherry (American Black) This wood can vary in color from light to reddish brown. Cherry has a fine grain pattern, is close pored and accepts clear finishes, such as varnish, very well. It is easy to work with and is a popular wood for furniture making.

Chestnut This grayish-brown wood has lighter streaks; it is durable and easy to work. Currently it is usually available only in a "wormy" pattern, although there used to be a few additional varieties of chestnut. It is a hardwood with an open grain.

The natural rich color of cherry wood is one of the reasons it is popular. It is also strong, has attractive grain, and finishes well.

Cypress Another wood used primarily outdoors, where particular resistance to decay is desired, is cypress. It is available in shades from brown to almost black and with red overtones. The wood can feel oily to the touch and, while easy to work, it is not the kind of wood one normally considers for items inside the house.

Ebony The color of this wood ranges from deep brown to black; ebony logs are occasionally streaked with lighter colors. Ebony is a strong, hard hardwood with close grain. It is an expensive wood, and it has limited availability. It may be found in wall paneling, as an inlay material, in some musical instruments, and some woodwork. It is a dense wood and is difficult to work.

Fir This wood is basically a tan or yellow with darker brown streaks. Its grain pattern is very prominent. It is a strong wood that is not that easy to work with. Because of its grain pattern, it is often covered with opaque finishes.

Gum Used more commonly in making veneer than as a building material for projects, gum is a reddish-brown, attractive wood. While it is not particularly strong, it can be used with success to build cabinets. Availability of the wood is limited. Gum is close grained—no filling is required.

Hickory A wood that is very hard and difficult to work with, hickory is surprisingly vulnerable to decay and insect infestation. It is seldom used for furniture or for household woodwork, but it is commonly used in tool handles.

Color is a major appeal of mahogany. The quality of the grain is enhanced by a fine, clear finish and a lusterous polish.

Mahogany (African or Honduras) This is considered one of the finest furniture woods. These days fine woods are very expensive and mahogany will carry a premium price.

Although mahogany is usually thought of as a reddish wood, you may find boards that range from a golden brown (Honduras) to a red brown (African). Mahogany boards are most commonly available in a golden brown. Although this wood is of medium hardness, it is very strong and is often used for furniture because of its attractive color and fine grain pattern. It accepts all types of finishes well, but it is an open-pore wood, so it must be filled before the finish can be applied.

Maple (True, Hard) Available in a variety of colors ranging from nearly white to red-brown, maple is available in various configurations. While maple is normally straight grained, it is also available in curly, burl and so-called "fiddleback" patterns, among others. Bird's Eye maple, for example, has a small swirling pattern and is used for interior paneling in the Rolls Royce. Maple is very tough, strong, hard and close grained—it takes finishes very well.

Oak There are two types of oak—red oak and white oak. As the name implies, red oak is red (actually a reddish tan or brown). White oak is lighter and is usually a grayish tan.

Oak is a very hard hardwood, and it is well known for its durability. Oak is used in furniture and flooring because it will stand up to long-term, heavy use and wear. However, it does have very large pores that must be well filled or the wood will not accept a stain or other finish well.

Pine is a plentiful and relatively inexpensive soft wood. The grain pattern is not prominent unless stained. Pine will accept many different finishes and may be matched to other woods.

Oak is a popular wood for furniture; it is often worked in carvings because the wood does not dent easily and stands up to wear.

Because oak is a very hard wood, it is difficult to work with. If you have ever attempted to drive a light nail into a piece of oak, this fact has been made abundantly clear. However, with the right tools and equipment you can work with it. The good looks, durability and strength of oak make it a popular wood for furniture, floors and woodwork.

Pine This softwood is one of the most popular furniture woods because it is plentiful, relatively cheap and easily finished. It is often white or cream colored, but the color can vary considerably from region to region and from species to species.

Pine comes in various grades, ranging from Clear, which is the best, through Select No. 1, 2, and 3 to Common pine. The Clear grades have no knots or blemishes; Select comes with a few; Common has the most. It is heartily suggested that you pick through the stack of boards at the lumber yard so that you can get the best of what is available. For example, under the Common grade heading you can find pieces that have varying degrees of blemishes, and you may get exactly what you need without having to buy the better grades.

Pine is normally available in an abundance of sizes. Furniture grades are available in "quarter stock" in many thicknesses and widths. Construction grades from Clear to Common are available in 1x2, 1x3, and 1x4 and then up to 1x18 in 1-inch increments. It is also available in standard 2x stock in all sizes and 4x stock in several sizes. The greatest advantage of this wood is, quite simply, that it is commonly available in so many grades and sizes.

Poplar A hardwood that is often finished to resemble more expensive woods such as mahogany and walnut, poplar is usually white or yellow and may have streaks of black. The heartwood has a greenish cast. Although it is a hardwood, poplar is relatively soft. It does not stand up to wear and tear as well as some of the other hardwoods. It is used mostly inside cabinets for partitions and drawer parts and as cross banding in plywood.

Redwood This expensive, reddish-brown stock is a big favorite for outdoor projects. It can be finished but if left unfinished, it will weather to a silvery gray. It is light and strong, has outstanding resistance to decay, is quite soft and easy to work with, and is used for sheet or plank paneling, woodwork, shelving and furniture.

Teak An Oriental wood that has been a fine furniture wood of great popularity, teak ranges dark yellow to dark brown in color. Teak has an open grain, is very hard and extremely expensive. It accepts clear finishes very well. Because of its natural strength and beauty, it is often given an oil finish. It is naturally resistant to wear and moisture;

The grain pattern of teak makes it an attractive furniture wood. Its natural resistance to moisture makes it popular for tables.

it is a favorite wood of shipbuilders.

Walnut (American Black) A favorite furniture wood, walnut is usually a chocolate brown color. The grain is prominent and is open pored. Walnut is of medium hardness. Much of the Commercial production is used for veneer so that boards are scarce and expensive.

This chair arm shows that walnut may be carved or turned. Usually available only in veneers, solid walnut furniture is rare.

VENEERS

It is estimated that veneers can be obtained in over 250 different woods. The length and width of the veneer sheets will vary according to the tree from which it is sliced. One prime source of wood veneer is Constantine's in the Bronx, New York, which sells hundreds of exotic and ordinary veneers. Knowing something about veneer is important to both the furniture finisher and the builder.

Veneers are extremely thin sheets of very fine wood. Standard furniture veneers are cut between 1/28 and 1/40

Veneering developed as a cabinetmaker's art. Fine veneering, such as in this 18th century highboy, is the mark of good furniture.

of an inch thick. They are used to cover furniture or other wood surfaces. Veneer became popular because of economics. It is far cheaper to cover a piece of furniture with a thin veneer of beautiful wood than to use solid stock throughout. Precise application and inlaying of fine veneers became the mark of the true craftsman in the 18th century. Veneered wood does not necessarily mean cheap furniture.

Fixing or Refinishing Veneered Surfaces

Before attempting to refinish any piece of furniture, examine it carefully to see if it is covered with veneer. The pieces may have a veneer layer that has been applied separately or it may be made with plywood with a fine wood veneer face. If there are no signs of boards being glued together, no seams, then the surface is veneered, and you should proceed slowly in finishing or refinishing it. Because it is very thin, veneer can be sanded through with the greatest of ease. Replacing sanded through veneer is a problem to be corrected, if possible

Patching veneer requires matching the wood grain and finish. This piece of veneer has been stained to match the veneered surface.

to correct it at all, by a professional refinisher.

You can also apply veneer to a piece of furniture. The technique is similar to applying plastic laminate, but it is the opinion of this writer that for many novice craftpersons, this installation is too chancy and difficult. It requires a great deal of patience. Veneer is, as mentioned, very thin and may arrive wrinkled, broken or cracked; it must be replaced or repaired carefully before use. The handing takes skill that is developed through practice. Because veneer is expensive and damage incidence can be high, the application simply may be too costly for the average person.

PLYWOOD CHARACTERISTICS

The plywood material we see today is very different from the material originally available under that term. At one time plywood had problems (such as the failure of the glue to hold the plies together) that made it of questionable dependability. This did not enhance its value to the furniture maker or the builder. Today, plywood has changed, and it now is a great asset to the builder; indeed many furniture makers like it better than solid stock. It comes in larger sizes so you do not have to join boards by edge-gluing, and it is easier to finish because it comes pre-sanded. It can be handled as if it were solid stock—finished and worked with power tools in almost the same way. There are, however, some joints that can be made with solid stock that cannot be made with plywood.

Plywood Structure

Plywood consists of a face and back veneer, and a core, or filler, in between. Commonly, this core is inexpensive, thin wood sheets glued together with exterior glue for exterior plywood or interior glue for interior. The layers (plies) are laid at right angles to one another, giving the sheets extraordinary strength.

There are, in addition to exterior and interior plywood, two types of hardwood and softwood plywood. Hardwood plywood has either one or both sides covered with a veneer of an attractive hardwood such as birch, mahogany or walnut. A softwood plywood has one or both faces of a softwood like redwood, fir, or pine, for example. Hardwood plywood

Lumber core plywood has a solid core faced with two or more layers of thin plies. The exterior plies may be of furniture grade wood.

Plywood may have as few as three alternating plies of wood. This sheet combines solid wood plies and compressed fiber layers.

is normally used for furniture or cabinetry because the beauty and color of its grain will enhance the look of the object. Softwood plywood, commonly used in construction, is more easily located than hardwood.

Plywood Grades (Softwood)
The quality of the face veneers—their condition—is indicated by letters: "A" designating the best and "D" the worst. The A face plywood is free from blemishes; it is absolutely clear and free of knots or visible mars and, after a light sanding, is ready for finishing. Grade "B" will have a few defects but the knotholes will have been cut out and the area patched. Grade "C" Plugged has repaired knotholes. Grade C has unfilled knotholes and checks (splits). Grade D plywood often has large knotholes. There is also a Grade "N" (natural) that designates furniture quality wood veneer free of all defects. This must be special ordered and has limited availability in most areas.

Analyze your project to determine the plywood quality you will need. If you are building or replacing hidden shelves or cabinet partitions, you do not need A-A grade. Plywood comes with A-A, A-B, A-C, A-D, B-B, B-C, B-D, C-C, and C-D sides. Buy the lowest grade that will meet your needs.

Plywood Grades (Hardwood)
The exposed plies for this type of plywood are designated as Premium, Good, Sound and Backing. A Premium sheet may have two sides of Premium veneer or one side Premium and one of backing grade. The latter plywood is suitable for a piece which will have one side hidden from view.

The next category is a Custom sheet. This allows a combination of Premium and Backing grades, or a Premium and Good side for two exposed faces.

The final category is Economy grade. This permits faces to be combined as Good and Backing, Good and Sound, or two faces Sound.

The Premium and Good designations indicate that the exposed surface is nearly perfect and suitable for a clear finish. The only difference between the two grades is that Premium grade allows only small, inconspicuous patches, while the Good grade allows larger, but carefully matched patches.

The Good grade allows mismatching of grain but not of color. Sound grade is intended for a painted finish.

Choosing Plywood
The following recommendations are based on long experience. For cabinet making or for furniture parts that will be stained or covered with a clear finish so that the wood will show (i.e., the color and grain will be exposed), the top, Premium or A, grade is recommended. If both sides will show, the A-A or possibly A-B or Premium should be used. The use of Custom grade, A-C or A-D depends on how attractive you feel the back or hidden face should be.

If you intend to apply paint to the plywood, then grades B-B and B-D should be used. If you wish, you may

even obtain a plywood that has been primed at the factory.

Handling Plywood Edges
Plywood can be worked easily with good power tools or hand tools, as needed. Because the face(s) of plywood are pre-sanded, there are no particular finishing problems. Except for the lighter sanding, you prepare and finish plywood as you would solid stock.

The only areas that present potential problems are the edges. Lumber core plywood has nearly solid board edges that may be handled in the same way as any solid wood. However, if the edges are exposed layers of plies, the appearance may be unattractive and you will want to hide them.

There are several ways to do this. One way is to build the items so the edges do not show. Use rabbet joints, butt joints or other joints in which the exposed plies cannot be seen.

If you have the right power equipment, you can rip thin strips of wood from solid stock of the same wood as the plywood face and tack them in place with brads. If you have the time and patience, you can miter all the joints to hide the plies.

Perhaps the most popular way to finish plywood edges is with a veneer tape. This material comes in a roll and is applied to the exposed edges with contact cement. Instructions vary a little from brand to brand, but all are applied essentially the same.

If you simply are going to paint the plywood, there is no need to use any special edge finishing techniques or material. Instead, choose one of the many wood puttys, either in powder or semi-solid form, and apply it as directed to fill and smooth the edges. The putty will seal the edges of the plywood and keep the fibers from absorbing excess amounts of paint. The filled and painted edges will look like the rest of the plywood.

OTHER MATERIALS
You may encounter a variety of other materials in finishing and refinishing work. These include particleboard, hardboard and flakeboard. There is only one way to finish these. Paint them. The primary concern in this book will be handling the finishing and refinishing of wood only.

2
Sanding and Abrasives

One adage known to furniture finishers is that the start makes the finish; the start of furniture finishing is sanding. There are many grades and types of sandpaper available and many techniques for using sandpaper.

CHOICES IN SANDPAPER

Although referred to as a "sandpaper", this abrasive material no longer consists of sand bonded to paper. There is a wide array of grits and papers available, but the paper may not be paper at all. Manufacturers prefer to label sandpaper as a coated abrasive. Any number of abrasives are used to create the product, which is available in different sizes and shapes for both hand and power-assisted finishing work.

Types of Sandpapers

Flint The least expensive sandpaper is flint paper. Flint is a gray mineral. It wears down quickly and is used mainly in paint removing. Because paint will clog the grit on the paper and reduce its usefulness before the paper is worn smooth, pieces have to be discarded frequently, so it is advisable to use as inexpensive a paper as possible.

Garnet The grit on garnet sandpaper is much harder than on flint paper and is more suitable for use in woodworking.

Emery This abrasive is recognizable by its distinctive black color. This is still fairly widely used as a metal abrasive, although more recently developed abrasives may be more effective.

Aluminum Oxide This probably is the more popular sandpaper abrasive for furniture finishing and refinishing. The oxide is reddish in color, and its grit is very sharp and much harder than the first three papers listed here. While it is popular for use on wood, it can also be used on metal. Aluminum oxide is more expensive than the other sandpaper, but it lasts so long that it is often cheaper to use in the long run.

Silicon Carbide This is the hardest, sharpest sandpaper of all. The bluish black material cuts extremely well and is commonly used for such tough jobs as finishing metal, glass or for floor sanding.

SANDPAPER CLASSIFICATIONS
Grit

The grit, or the particles that are adhered to the backing material, are each identified by a number of labeling systems. There is a so-called "Retail System" that carries word descriptions (coarse, medium, fine). There is an old system that identified the papers by numbers that run from 10/0 to 4½ to reflect increasing coarseness. The currently used "Industrial System" identifies grit with numbers from 600 down through 12. In the Industrial System, the grit specified is coarser as the numbers become smaller. The accompanying chart presents the three systems.

Density

Another factor that affects the way sandpaper functions is the density of the grit—how close together the granules are on the backing. There are two classifications: Closed Coat and Open Coat. Closed coat indicates that the grit material blankets 100 percent of the surface; open coat indicates that the grit covers from 50 percent to 70 percent of the surface. Open coat may not look very "open", especially when the abrasive is of a fine density.

Generally, closed coat sandpapers are designed for fine finishing. Closed coat paper tends to clog quickly. Wood particles are caught and fill the spaces between the pieces of grit. Because open coat sandpapers do not clog as easily they are a better choice when you do a first sanding to remove a lot of material from the wood. The usable life and cutting action of any sandpaper can be extended and improved by rapping the paper on a hard surface from time to time to dislodge wood particles.

Adhesives

There is another component in sandpaper: glue. The grit is held by any one of a variety of glues.

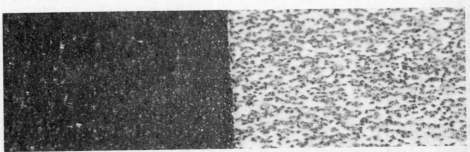

Closed coat sandpaper is largely covered by abrasive. Open coat is less densely covered.

SANDPAPER GRADES

Retail system	Old System	Industrial	Common Uses
Extra Fine/Superfine	—	600	Used wet on stone, plastic,
	—	500	metal—not wood. Between
	10/0	400	finish coats on furniture.
	9/0	360	
		320	
Very Fine	8/0	280	Polishing wood between coats.
	7/0	240	Many finishers use wet.
	6/0	220	
Fine	5/0	180	Smoothing bare wood; i.e., final
	4/0	150	smoothing before finish is
	3/0	120	applied.
Medium	2/0	100	Shaping wood, first sanding of
	1/0 or 0	80	soft woods.
	½	60	
Coarse	1	50	Removing paint. Rough sanding
	1½	40	and shaping of wood.
Very Coarse	2	36	First sanding of bare wood
	2½	30	floors.
	3	24	
Extra Coarse	3½	20	Sanding painted floors.
	4	16	
	4½	12	

Hide glue is used on sandpapers intended for light to medium work. Hide glue is not waterproof, so the paper cannot be used on a wet surface. Thermosetting resin is used to secure grit on papers where the work is harder, such as floor sanding. Waterproof resin bonds grit to backings that are waterproof. Such glue allows the paper to be used with oil or water for extra fine and smooth finishing.

Weight and Backing

The backing of the sandpaper may range from paper or cloth to a combination of cloth and paper or even a plastic material. The paper comes in various weights, which lend certain advantages or disadvantages.

A weight paper is the lightest of all and the first to wear through. Use it only for touching up wood lightly.

Moving up the scale, C weight is stiffer and stronger than A weight and is used for coarse machine sanding. D weight is even stronger and is for heavy machine sanding. E weight is the strongest of all. It is designed to be used in conjunction with very coarse grits of sandpaper and is used with floor sanding machines or belt sanders.

In the cloth backings, the weights are J weight and X weight. J is the lighter of the two and is used on curves and other shapes. The X weight cloth is designed for coarse grit abrasives used with a belt sander.

Fiber weight backings are very heavy and are not needed by the do-it-yourselfer for any of the projects discussed in this book.

OTHER ABRASIVES

There are two powdered stone abrasives commonly used in furniture finishing and refinishing. These abrasives are applied with an oil. Depending on the situation, you may mix the powdered stone with lubricating oil and apply with a rag, or you may dip the rag in the oil and then in the stone before applying.

Pumice This is a lava. The stone is porous and relatively soft. When pumice is crushed to a powder, the stone is a medium to fine abrasive.

Rottenstone This is a decomposed limestone, a form of sedimentary rock. This material crushes to a very fine abrasive powder. Applied with oil, rottenstone is used to create or to restore a smooth finish to furniture.

Either of these abrasives may be used to create the glassy finish of a French polish.

STEEL WOOL

Steel wool is also used for smoothing wood. It comes, like sandpaper, in a variety of grades. Each has a number and name description. Following is a brief description of each grade and common uses.

0000 This is the finest grade of steel wood usually available. It creates a satin smooth finish on fine woods. It is used for such jobs as rubbing down shellacs, lacquers and varnishes, waxes and oils. It is also used for cleaning delicate instruments.

000 Extra Fine This is used for both cabinet work and auto finishing as well as to remove minor cracks or checks and burn marks in a finish. This grade also performs well in removing paint spots and splatters. It is also the steel wool grade used to polish metals, such as aluminum, copper, brass and zinc.

00 Fine This grade is used to cut gloss finishes of paint to a semi-gloss. It is also desirable for cleaning and polishing wood floors, plastic tile and terrazo. A varnish remover is applied with 00 steel wool to remove old finishes.

0 Medium/Fine This is a grade not widely used in woodworking. It is primarily used for cleaning aluminum, copper, brass, or zinc and many metal objects such as barbecues, pots and pans and for removing rust.

1 Medium This grade is used to prepare wood for a first coat of paint. It is also used with soap and water to clean various flooring materials such as rubber, asphalt, linoleum and resilient floors.

2 Medium Coarse This grade is used to clean rust and dirt from garden tools, glass, brick, metal and stone. It is not often used on wood.

3 Coarse This grade is used to remove old paint and varnish. After the remover has caused the paint or varnish to liquify, 3 coarse steel wool can be rubbed on the surface to loosen the remaining paint.

BASIC SANDING PROCEDURES

You should always start a job with the smoothest usable grade of abrasive material. If you start with material that is coarser than necessary, you will cut small grooves in the surface. These will have to be removed in subsequent sandings. This means more work for you and less chance of a complete success in your finishing project.

Achieving a Smooth Finish

To prepare bare wood, follow the steps given below in order to achieve a fine, smooth surface suitable for application of a clear finish.

Step 1: Use Progressively Smoother Papers Start sanding with a 220 or 280 paper. If the wood is a softwood, use a 220 paper. If you are finish sanding a hardwood, use the 280 or finer papers. Wipe the dust off the surface regularly and use a tack rag, a cloth pretreated with a gummy material, to get the wood clean of all loose dust and grit. Keep sanding until the surface is as smooth as you wish. If you intend to paint the surface with enamel, the smoothness achieved with a 150 paper should be good enough.

Step 2: Raising the Grain At some point, it will seem that you have sanded the wood as smooth as possible. At this point you must "raise the grain". To do this, soak a rag with water and dampen the sanded surfaces. Let the wood dry at least 24 hours. Run your

What is usually called sandpaper may be made of various abrasive substances adhered to either paper or cloth backing. Type of abrasive, grit and density are usually marked on the back.

hand over the wood. If you feel a fine fuzz, the water has expanded the wood and the grain has been raised. Rub the surface gently with a fine sandpaper to take off the "Whiskers". Repeat this procedure and, if necessary, keep repeating it until no grain is raised.

Step 3: Using a Sanding Sealer You may achieve an even smoother finish by using a sanding sealer. These are available in paint stores and come with instructions for application. Such

sealers are also used over filler material so that after wood is filled, application of a final clear finish does not lift the filler. It is also used over raw wood to prevent excessive absorption of stain. Some finishers use it under final finish coats.

The sanding sealer you buy in the store is not cheap. You can make your own by mixing one part clear shellac with four parts denatured alcohol. Brush it on. When the mixture dries, do the final finish sanding.

This sheet shows that this medium weight, open coat paper is covered with aluminum oxide. It is good for a first sanding of soft wood.

Use your fingers to check the progress of your work. Wipe the surface with a tack rag and then run your hand along the wood to determine the degree of smoothness you have achieved.

SANDING BY HAND

For most finishers and refinishers, hand sanding is the technique of choice because the results can be controlled better. Also, hand sanding is unquestionably safer than machine sanding.

Achieving the Desired Smoothness
The object of sanding is to smooth the wood. The final character of the smooth surface will be dictated by the final finish chosen. If you plan to paint the piece with enamel, you need not sand as smoothly as you would if you were going to use a clear finish. The enamel finish will be glasslike as long as the sanding is reasonably smooth and the paint is applied with careful brushwork. A clear finish requires an extremely smooth surface for a high quality surface.

The best choice for someone hand sanding a piece of furniture or trim is an open coat garnet or aluminum oxide paper. This should produce the desired surface.

Sight is not as important as touch in evaluating smoothness; the hand is a more sensitive instrument. Run your hand over the wood regularly to check your progress and the smoothness of the surface. Wipe or blow away the dust frequently. Dust will not only inhibit the cutting action of the sandpaper by clogging the grit, but you may inadvertently grind the dust into the pores of the wood. Dust forced into the wood will interfere with even application of stain.

USING A SANDING BLOCK
You will undoubtedly get a smoother finish and find the job easier if you use a sanding block when you sand a flat surface. There are commercially made sanding blocks available, but it is simple to cut a 3 inch piece of 2x4 stock to use as a block. Glue a thin piece of felt or foam rubber to one of the large faces of the block. This is important. When you sand, dust can work its way between the piece of sandpaper and the block; without any

A sanding block will provide even pressure when sanding a flat surface. Wrap sandpaper around block and attach with thumb tacks.

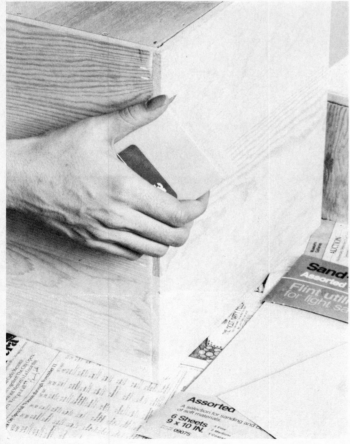

You may prefer to buy a commercially manufactured sanding block. The block creates a better sanding surface and protects your hand.

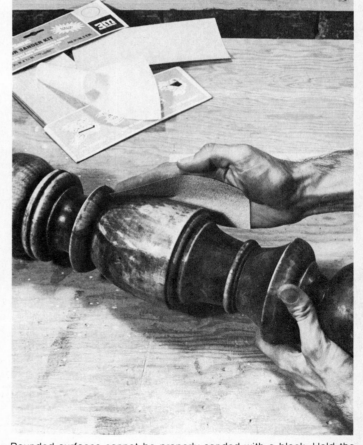

Rounded surfaces cannot be properly sanded with a block. Hold the paper with your hand and apply steady pressure to the turned wood.

''give'' in the block, the dust could create an uneven surface that could scratch the wood.

Cut a piece of 9x11 inch sandpaper into six pieces. Wrap a piece of sandpaper around the block and hold it in place with thumbtacks or roofing nails pushed into the sides of the block. Change the paper as needed.

If you are sanding a curved surface, glue felt or rubber around a section of dowel or a broomstick and wrap sandpaper over the rubber. This tool will help you smooth inward curves. In some situations, of course, you will not be able to use either a block or a piece of dowel. If this is the case, fold sandpaper into a small rectangle and apply it to the surface with your hand. Keep your strokes at an even pressure. Changes of pressure will result in your creating an uneven surface on the wood.

If you must sand a spot where it is difficult to manipulate the paper, glue a piece of cardboard to the sandpaper as a backing. This will give rigidity to the paper, making it easier for you to handle the paper and to apply even pressure.

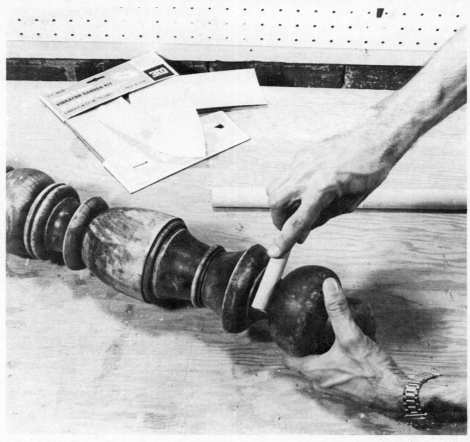

A curved block can be made by wrapping a piece of sandpaper around a wooden dowel. Use dowels of appropriate size for different areas.

If you must use sandpaper without a block, you can control the pressure better if you glue a piece of cardboard to the back of the sandpaper.

SANDING WITH A MACHINE

Although hand sanding is of primary concern to the refinisher, there are some jobs that may be done by machine. There are basically three kinds of sanding machines: the disc, the belt and the finishing sander. The first two have very limited use, if any at all, for the wood finisher.

THE DISC SANDER

A disc sander has, as its name indicates, a revolving disc. It is used to take off very rough finishes. It is difficult to control depth of the sanding cut using this device. The disc cuts across the grain, which is usually not suggested when sanding furniture. It can scratch the surface and dig gouges that are difficult to remove.

Although not useful for furniture sanding, any drill may be adapted for disc sanding. The disc sander will cut through paint quickly.

THE BELT SANDER

The belt sander is a heavy duty machine with a revolving belt. It is sometimes used in finishing furniture or trim, but it only can be used on flat surfaces. It cannot sand anything carved or shaped, and it can be risky to use because it works at such high speed. It is capable of taking off great quantities of material before you are aware of the extent of the sanding. It is also a heavy machine, which means it is awkward to hold a belt sander against a piece of vertical trim.

If you do use a belt sander, take care to keep the machine moving constantly along the surface; if the sander rests in one place, it will cut deeply into the surface very quickly. It is also

important to be careful when using the machine near the edge of a piece; in an instant it can round off edges you do not want rounded off.

The belt sander will sand any flat surface well. It must be kept moving at all times to prevent uneven wearing away of the surface.

THE FINISHING SANDER

The logical machine sander for the do-it-yourself wood refinisher is the finishing sander. This machine uses a rectangular pad and precut pieces of sandpaper. The action of the sander is either straight line (back and forth) or orbital. Most finishing sanders are orbital; however, some come with both actions. A combination pattern sander has a lever that allows you to use either straight-line or orbital sanding action.

All of these machines, like most portable power tools, are available with all-plastic housings; they are dou-

ble-insulated to guard against electrical shock. Many models also come with dustbags and vacuum action. This feature reduces the irritation and mess of sawdust in the air and around the shop.

Using a Finishing Sander

The straight line action of a sander is slow, but it produces a smoother finish than the orbital action. Although the orbital does go against the grain in its round and round action, most workers end up satisfied with the smoothness of the finish it produces.

The secret of using a finishing sander is not to press down on the machine but to let the weight of the unit do the work. Pressing inhibits the sanding action of the machine; restriction of the movement may damage the machine motor.

If you are sanding vertical trim, the weight of the machine will not be exerted on the surface. In this case you will have to apply a little pressure, but you must be mindful not to exert too much.

When using a finishing sander—or a belt sander—you will use various sandpapers, starting with a relatively coarse grit and ending with a fine paper to produce the smooth finish you want.

The finishing sander is for use on fine woods and furniture. Even if you will do final sanding by hand, the finishing sander will be useful in preparing the wood for the hand work.

3
Small Repairs to Wood

If you are not refinishing a piece but are concerned with preserving the basic finish of your furniture and other wood, probably your main interest is removal and repair of scratches and stains. It should be noted that no repair you can make will be perfect—absolutely invisible. It takes years of experience before a refinisher acquires the skill and subtlety to create an imperceptible repair. However, you should be able to repair mars and scratches well enough so that the repair will not be seen easily. Remember, however, that a poorly done repair often is more objectionable than the original scratch or mar.

In finishing and refinishing, however, there are also repairs that must be made before the process can be completed. Making repairs may seem an unlikely part of a refinishing process, but it is wiser and easier to remove scratches and fill dents before you finish the wood. It is always risky to attempt major repairs after the finishing is completed. Check the wood thoroughly before you begin to apply the finish. Later repairs may leave new scratches. Indeed, doing a small job first may prevent the need for a big job later.

CAUTION: TOXIC PRODUCTS
Handle all refinishing materials with great care. Read all warning labels and follow precautions. Many products used by the refinisher are toxic and volatile. Never attempt any refinishing project unless you are in a well-ventilated area. Some products are toxic even through the skin; wear protective gloves. In some cases, heart, lung, liver and brain damage are possible unless products are used carefully. Respect and observe all health and safety rules, and use caution. Do not use a product with a known toxicity level for more than part of a day. It is better to have a project take longer than expected than to risk any damage to your health.

Read and follow all directions carefully.

Small mars, scratches and stains can be removed as part of basic furniture maintenance. A high polish can be restored with rottenstone and oil rubbed in the direction of the grain.

REPAIRING SHALLOW SCRATCHES

Finished furniture often acquires both shallow and deep scratches. Scratches are considered shallow when they have not penetrated the finish to the wood.

REPAIRING SHALLOW SCRATCHES

The scratches are often very apparent because the surface finish cracks to a fine powder in the scratch. First, clean the scratch. This may make it less noticeable. If this is not sufficient try to hide it with colorant.

Suggested Coloring Aids

If the finish or wood of the piece is walnut and the scratch is small, rub the meaty portion of a walnut, a Brazil nut or a butternut along the scratch to color in the scratch. For mahogany of a brown or cherry color, apply old iodine that has become dark with age. For red mahogany, fresh iodine is often a good colorant. If the piece is maple and finished in a reddish color, you can try old iodine thinned by 50 percent with denatured alcohol. Apply the liquids with a narrow (0 or 00) artist's brush or Q-tip. After the colorant is dry, wax and buff the piece as required. Be careful to avoid dropping any iodine on surrounding areas.

Liquid Colors

You can find a wide variety of commercially prepared liquid colors in well-stocked paint stores. There are aniline stains that come in many different wood colors. They are sold in small bottles that have a built-in applicator. You may have to buy and combine two or more colors to get the closest color match. As with all other color application, apply it to an inconspicuous part of the furniture first to check the color match.

Polishes

There also are "scratch-removing" furniture polishes available. These are pigmented oil-base products. The pigment in the polish penetrates the scratches and hides them. They do not make permanent changes, but do hide most scratches temporarily and make the surface appear smooth.

Emergency Repairs To Shallow Scratches

If a piece of furniture receives a noticeable but shallow scratch that you have to hide quickly, you can use ordinary shoe polish to color it in. Black shoe polish works on black lacquered wood, cordovan works on mahogany, brown on walnut and tan on light woods. Apply it with a Q-tip. If you discover that the shoe polish you use is not the proper color after you have applied it, remove it with naphtha. If you have time, try to test the color by applying the polish to an inconspicuous part of the furniture. When the polish is dry you can buff it to a shine, use furniture polish, or wax over it in a normal fashion.

Another device that is useful in hiding scratches is an almond stick. It can be used to disguise scratches very well. Zenith-Tibet is a manufacturer of one almond stick.

One excellent scratch "remover" is a Brazil or other nut. The natural oils in the nut will cover the mark and color the wood.

Rub the nutmeat across the wood, in the direction of the grain. The full effect of the treatment may not be noticed for a few hours.

A scratch that cuts through the finish to the wood but is not deep enough to require filling may be covered with color.

Liquid color, iodine, or "scratch removing polish" applied to the scratch will hide the mar until more extensive refinishing is needed.

A "emergency only" repair may be made by covering a scratch with a shoe polish that matches the color of the finished wood.

REPAIRING MAJOR SCRATCHES AND DENTS

A major scratch is one that goes through the finish to the wood. Repairing a scratch of this type requires more than simple cosmetic work.

USING COLORING STICKS

On finished wood, the simplest solution is to use coloring sticks. These sticks look like crayons and even have the consistency of hard crayons. They come in a wide variety of wood colors and are available at paint stores. However, they are only effective if the scratch is still relatively shallow.

Before using the wood color stick, clean the scratch out with naphtha and use a razor to scrape all loose material away. Rub the stick across the scratch, working along the length

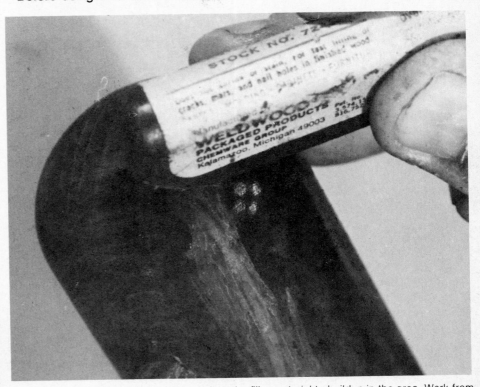

Rub the crayon across the scratch and allow the filler material to buildup in the area. Work from one end to the other, filling the scratch completely and overlapping the edges.

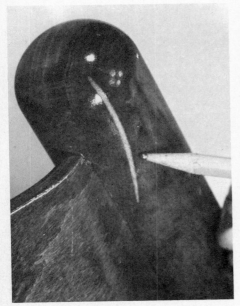

A scratch that cuts into the wood slightly can be filled with colored "crayons". Left unfilled, the scratch will be obvious.

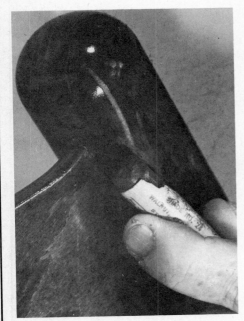

Filler crayons come in colors to match various wood finishes. You may find one that matches or you may have to combine two colors.

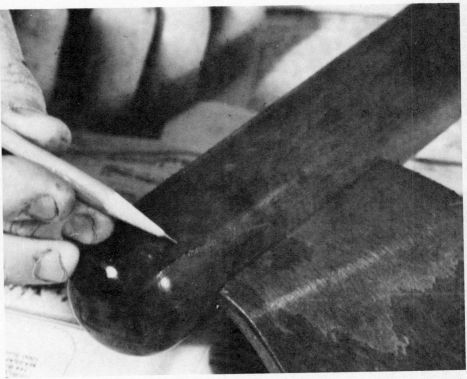

When the scratch is filled, smooth the area with a finger or a tool and rub the material smooth. Buff lightly to polish. Do not apply heavy pressure or you will remove the soft filler.

of the scratch. Work the material left in the scratch until it is level, using your finger or a putty knife. When the scratch is filled, rub it with a soft cloth. This is not really a permanent repair for a heavily used surface. You may have to repeat the application in a few months.

USING LACQUER OR SHELLAC STICKS

One alternative is a lacquer or shellac stick. These short, rectangular sticks of solid lacquer or shellac come in a variety of wood colors. They are applied by melting the stick and letting the melted lacquer or shellac drip into the scratch or gouge.

Application Procedures

You must use a clean flame from an alcohol lamp or canned heat to melt the stick. Other flame sources will produce soot, which will discolor the material. When you buy the stick, also purchase a thin, spatula-style applicator.

Step 1: Heating the Material Hold the tip of the applicator in the flame. When it is hot, wipe the tip on 00 steel wool, to clean it. Then apply the tip immediately to the end of the lacquer or shellac stick.

Step 2: Applying the Lacquer or Shellac Hold the stick a half inch above the scratch. Let the heated lacquer or shellac drip into the scratch, and smooth the material with the applicator.

Repeat the heating procedure, wiping the applicator on 00 steel wool then on a cloth before melting more shellac to drop into the scratch. Keep repeating the process, gradually building up coats of lacquer or shellac until the level of the material is slightly above the surface of the wood.

Step 3: Smoothing the Surface Let the lacquer or shellac harden. Then hold a new, single-blade razor vertically to the patch, to scrape the shellac or lacquer level with the surface. If the patch has spread beyond the scratched area, use denatured alcohol and a Q-tip to carefully remove the excess.

When hard, rub the shellac or lacquer with 000 steel wool. Wipe the spot with a dry rag; then rub the surface with a tack rag to remove all steel wool particles. A tack rag is a cloth pretreated so it will pick up all dust on a surface.

Step 4: Blending the Patch Of course, you will want to insure that the patch blends in with the surrounding area as much as possible. If you use a shellac stick, and the surface finish is shellac, you should be finished. If the stick is shellac and the surface finish is wax, apply a coat of wax to hide either the shellac or lacquer stick filler. You may wish to polish the shellac patch with pumice with oil in order to bring up the gloss. If the finish is high gloss lacquer, you can dab on a bit of lacquer with an artist's brush after the patch is smooth and dry. This should bring the spot to the gloss of surrounding area.

USING WOOD FILLERS

Although shellac and lacquer sticks are what most professionals prefer, it is sometimes difficult for the inexperienced refinisher to use them effectively. Many of the wood fillers available are much easier to use.

These materials, which have a putty-like consistency, are uncolored as well as in wood colors that can be mixed or colored.

Fillers are applied essentially like putty, with a scraper or putty knife. There are enough differences between the products that you should read and follow label instruction for whatever products you buy. Do not just trust your memory from the last use, or for any "similar" product.

Observe all label directions and warnings. Many wood fillers are toxic if not handled correctly. You can assume any finishing or refinishing product has some degree of hazard connected with its use.

APPLICATION PROCEDURES

Whatever product you use, do not spread it beyond the gouged or scratched area. Any filler that gets on the finished surface is usually difficult to remove. If you do not remove it, the filler will show when final finishing is done.

Fixing Scratches With Wood Filler

Wood filler is useful for repairing a scratch or hole that is particularly deep. In new wood (unfinished) just fill

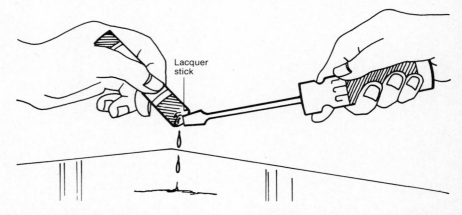

A lacquer stick will make a more permanent repair. You must melt the material with hot metal. The lacquer will harden in the scratch. Overfill the scratch to assure complete repair.

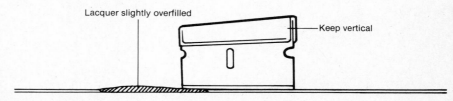

Lacquer slightly overfilled — Keep vertical

When the material is hard, use a single-edge razor blade to remove the material that stands above the surface of the wood. Buff the repair with 000 steel wool and clean with a tack rag.

the scratch with the filler, let it harden and apply the stain and finish you want. (See Chapter 5.) For finished wood, you can fill the scratch and match the existing finish or, if you wish, you can also fill the damaged spot to three-quarters with the wood filler and fill the rest of the area with shellac stick.

Using Wood Filler To Repair A Broken Corner

Sometimes the corner of a piece of furniture becomes worn down or broken off and must be repaired with wood filler. In this case, you must not only fill the crack, but also must create a support to hold the filler in position until it has set.

One way to build a form is to use tongue depressors held in place with masking tape. Then use wood filler to make the repair. When the material

has set, cut the filler to 1/32 inch of above adjacent area size, remove the form and the area is ready to be sanded smooth and as desired.

SCRATCHES AND STAINS ON NEW WOODS

No matter how much care you exercise when working with new wood—whether building an item yourself, handling unfinished furniture, or just stripping an old piece of furniture down to raw wood—a number of problems are likely to occur. Many are the same kinds of problems that occur with finished furniture. Here are the most common problems that may beset raw wood and what should be done about them.

Handling Scratches and Dents

If the new wood is scratched or dented in handling, you can use any of the

methods detailed in this chapter to solve the problem. If the scratch is very minor, normal sanding preparatory to finishing should remove it.

Stains and Discolorations

New wood, because it is unprotected, is particularly susceptible to oil and grease stains. A detailed procedure for removing these stains is given in Chapter 4. (It should be noted that finished furniture can also be penetrated by oil and grease; the method for removing these is given in Chapter 4.)

Dark Spots, Discolorations

New wood often suffers from stains from foodstuffs and soil. See Chapter 4 for the removal methods.

Dents occur when the wood fibers have been compressed but not actually broken or cut. If examination reveals a dent rather than a break, you should try to make the wood fibers swell so that they become level with the surface.

DENTS

A good tool to raise a dent is an ordinary household iron set at pressing temperature. This technique does not produce instant results, but it works.

If you are trying to repair a dent in bare wood, you do not have to do any special preparation. If the dent is in furniture that already has a finish, wipe the area with a cotton swab dampened in a mild solution of Soilax or similar product to remove any polish or wax. This will allow the steam to reach the wood fibers more easily.

To protect the wood from the iron, place a piece of folded cheese cloth or a blanket edge over the area. Dampen the cloth very lightly; if you have a steam iron you do not need to dampen the cloth. Place the cloth over the dent and move the iron along the dent. Do not hold the iron over the dent for more than a few seconds at a time or you will soften the finish and scorch the wood. Gradually, the moisture should work its way into the wood fibers and cause them to swell back into shape. If the raw wood fibers show, you can handle the dent like a scratch, as discussed earlier.

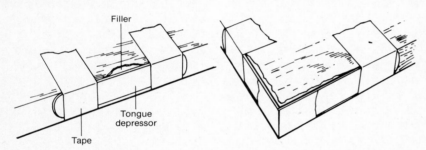

Wood filler can be used to make major repairs to damaged edges. Tongue depressors may be used as "forms" for the filler to control the shape and extent of the filler repairs.

A dent in wood can be raised with careful application of heat and moisture. Use a steam iron set on a piece of terrycloth or other soft material to raise the wood fibers.

REPAIRING LOOSE OR DAMAGED VENEER

Veneer can develop a variety of problems. Some are simple to repair; some are more complicated. A veneered piece may have come unglued and may be reapplied without great difficulty, but patching a cracked or broken section requires some skill and painstaking care.

Veneer becomes loose for a variety of reasons. Veneer may pull free of the adhesive if subject to excessive moisture or heat. The glue holding the veneer may simply be old, and it has lost its holding power. Many animal and fish glues used until recent years dried out and came off. Because veneer usually becomes loose at the edge, it is not difficult to do this.

REGLUING LOOSE VENEER

First, use a nail file, a single-edge razor blade, Exacto or other fine-bladed knife to scrape out all the old glue, dirt, or other foreign matter that may have become lodged under the veneer. Use an ear syringe, or similar device, to blow all dust and debris from the unglued area under the veneer.

Use a razor blade or nail file to carefully raise the veneer as far as you can. Do not lift it too far or it will crack. Use a toothpick to apply white glue under the veneer. Cover as much of the entire underneath area as possible; press the veneer down. As you press, glue will squeeze out; wipe this away immediately. Place heavy books or other padded weight on the area to hold the veneer in place until the glue sets. Although white glue is water soluble, use sandpaper carefully to remove any glue that may squeeze out under pressure and dry. Use a grade that will

cut through the glue. Stop before you sand the veneer. If you wipe the excess off with a damp rag, the edge of the veneer may pull free again. Put nothing between the veneer and the weight.

FIXING A BUBBLE IN VENEER

A bubble is a more serious problem than loose veneer. This occurs when an area becomes wet or is overheated and the adhesive breaks down. The veneer lifts up and creates a bubble. If you do not repair the bubble, the veneer is likely to split.

If the veneer has not yet cracked, cut the bubble down the center with a razor so you can poke under the veneer. Make the cut parallel to the grain.

Use a small cotton swab, applied carefully, to scrap away all the dried glue. Then blow as much of the foreign matter as possible from under the bubble. After cleaning, apply white glue under the veneer with a toothpick or fine wire. Place a piece of wax paper over the bubble and press it down with heavy books. If the books do not press the bubble flat, dampen the veneer slightly and apply more weight.

Once the glue has set, remove the books and peel off the wax paper. Finish the surface as required. If there is any glue on the surface, use a damp rag to remove any residue of glue. Very little should seep out of the slit in the bubble.

REPLACING VENEER BROKEN AT THE EDGE

Veneer is also susceptible to chipping at the edge. It is likely that if a piece

has chipped off, it is long lost. However, if you still have the chip, you can resecure it. If the piece is lost, you may be able to find a replacement in a piece of old furniture in a junk shop or at a second-hand store. Sometimes these shops have broken furniture sections; you may find an entire piece of furniture worth buying just for the veneer. A more direct source is Constantine's, a mail order house in the Bronx, New York. They sell a variety of veneer samples, one of which should match your piece of furniture. (At the time this manuscript was prepared, you could buy a box of fifty pieces of veneer for $7.95.)

If you have the old piece of veneer that has chipped off, simply clean the glue from the veneer and the base and resecure the veneer in place with white glue, following the method given above.

If you must use a replacement section, find a piece that matches as closely as possible both the color and grain of the surface. Cut a piece of veneer large enough to cover and slightly overlap the empty area. Lay this piece over the chipped section. Use a new razor and metal straightedge as a guide to cut through both the patch and the old veneer. This will produce an exact match between the edges of the old and new veneer. If possible, cut an oval patch. This will make the repair harder to distinguish.

Using a razor or razor knife, pry off the damaged veneer from the piece of furniture. When the area has been cleaned of all old veneer, glue and dirt, secure the patch—already cut with white glue. Press and weight it in place.

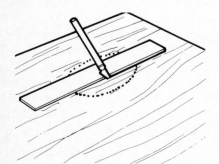

Use a sharp knife or a razor blade to cut the center of a veneer bubble. Cut on the grain to make the repair as invisible as possible.

Scrape out loose glue and debris. Use an syringe or baster to blow dust from under the veneer. Apply glue with toothpick or knife tip.

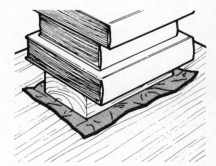

Roll bubble flat with rolling pin or other roller. Lay a piece of wax paper over the veneer and weight down the area with heavy books.

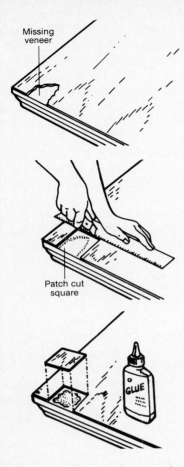

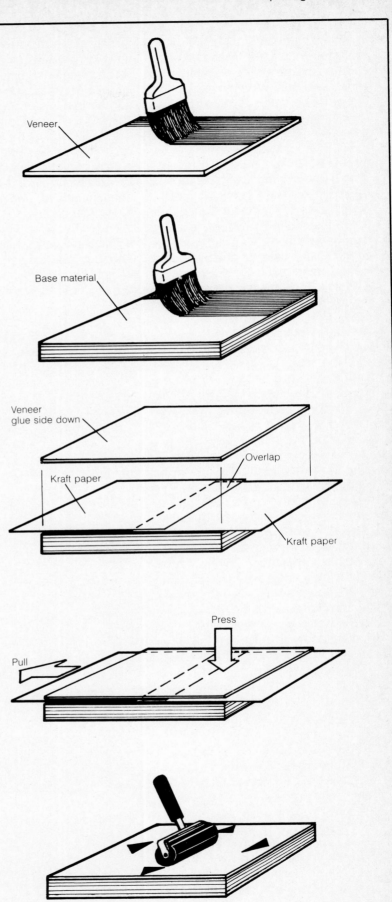

It is relatively easy to patch veneer at a straight edge. Cut a square or rectangular patch and fit it in place.

To assure fit, tape veneer over broken area and cut patch and excess around broken veneer in one stroke. Patch will be exact match.

REMOVING STAINS AND BLEMISHES

In addition to scratches and actual breaks in the wood, finished wood is subject to a variety of blemishes that can and should be removed. Among the most common are white marks, ink stains, candle wax, and stuck newsprint.

TAKING OUT WHITE MARKS

White marks appear on finished surfaces when a wet glass, a coaster or plates, or any hot object is placed on a surface and left—not necessarily a long time, either. In some cases, just contact may be enough to create a disfiguring problem.

White marks may be removed by using a mild abrasive made of damp ashes from ordinary cigars or cigarettes or with toothpaste. Make a paste with the ashes and a little water or a few drops of mineral oil. Dip a cotton swab into the mixture and rub the mark in the direction of the grain of the wood. Check your progress regularly; this should remove the mark quickly. Do not rub so hard that you make a deeper mark on the finish.

If the ash mixture does not work, the next stop is to try rottenstone. This is a gray, mild abrasive available at paint stores. Use with a mineral or linseed oil and a piece of felt or flannel cloth folded into a small pad.

Put the rottenstone in one saucer and the oil in another; dip the pad into the oil and then in the rottenstone. Rub the cloth across the mark following the wood grain. This combination is more abrasive than ash, so work carefully, slowly, and lightly.

The rottenstone and oil should remove the mark. If you apply enough pressure to dull the finish, then touch up the area with furniture polish or wax.

REMOVING INK STAINS

As stains go, ink is usually one of the worst. Although few people use liquid ink regularly these days, you may find an occasional use for it and all bottled ink can spill. Once spilled and set, it often cannot be removed and the entire piece of wood has to be refinished.

The best course is to try to blot up as much of the ink as possible as quickly as possible after the spill. Use a lot of toweling or other highly absorbant material, applied to the area and lifted straight up. Be careful not to rub or you may rub the ink in to the finish. After soaking up and blotting away as much of the ink as possible, apply wax or furniture polish. If there is an apparent dark area where the ink spilled, apply oil and rottenstone, as detailed above under ''Taking Out White Marks.''

REMOVING MILK STAINS

Although milk may seem harmless, it is not and will stain wood. Milk contains lactic acid and this does an un-

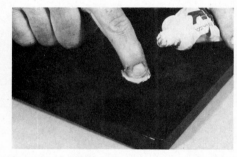
Small, light white marks from heat or moisture may be rubbed out with toothpaste.

More extensive white marks may be worked on with a paste of rottenstone and oil.

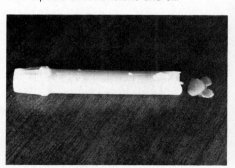
Candle wax dripped on wood should be removed as soon as the wax is hard.

expectedly quick job of eating into the finish on wood and producing a cloudy spot. Handle a milk spill on finished wood exactly like an ink spill. If a mark remains, remove the blemish with the methods detailed under ''Taking Out White Marks.'' Use either ash or rottenstone and oil.

REMOVING CANDLE WAX

When melted candle wax drips on a surface and hardens, the first step for removal is to make it harder. To do this, wrap an ice cube in thin plastic and apply the ice to the wax. The wax will harden. Very carefully, chip and scrap away the wax with a dull butter knife. Finally rub the area with a soft cloth and wax, and wipe with a dry cloth.

REMOVING STUCK NEWSPRINT

Newsprint, or other paper, can stick to a finished surface if a hot or wet object is laid on it. The stuck paper can be lifted easily if you soak it with vegetable oil. Most of the paper should lift right up. Use very fine steel wool to rub any residue off the surface.

Rub mark in the direction of the grain. Apply paste with cheesecloth or other soft rag.

Press an ice cube on the wax to harden. Lift wax off the wood with gentle pry action.

MAKING SIMPLE STRUCTURAL REPAIRS

Before you repair scratches or stains, you may need to repair some structural damage. Furniture components—legs or arms particularly—often become loose or broken from wear. If you have a piece of furniture with a loose or broken piece, you should make repairs as part of the refinishing job. The needed repairs may be very simple, such as tightening screws, but other repairs can require a bit of carpentry.

TIGHTENING LOOSE FASTENERS

If your piece of furniture has nails or screws that are loose, the simplest

Dowel-jointed chair stretchers often come loose from constant pressure and shrinkage that occurs in dry, heated air.

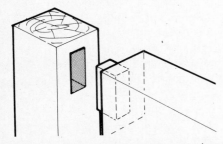

A mortise and tenon joint is similar to a dowel joint. The mortise (hole) and tenon are cut square or rectangular and fit precisely.

solution is to simply resecure them with a screwdriver or hammer. At the same time, check all the other fasteners. When one fastener becomes loose, other parts often are put under stress and become loose.

Enlarged Holes

In some cases you will find that screw or nail holes have become ragged or otherwise enlarged so that the fasteners no longer bite into the wood. If it is practical—i.e., you won't damage or mar the piece—you can use the next largest fastener. It will bite into new wood and grip securely.

Using a Filler If using a larger fastener means it will go through to an exposed surface, you can instead renew screw or nail holes. You do this by filling the hole with Plastic Wood or a similar product. Follow label directions and pack the material into the hole. Poke the material with a toothpick or nail to remove any air pockets. Level the putty flush with the surface of the wood. Let the filler material harden and then drive the screw or nail in place.

Using Wood Pieces Another option is to use cut-up slivers of wood, toothpicks, or headless wood matchsticks as a filler for the holes. Douse the filler pieces with white glue and pack them into the hole, tapping them in place with a hammer. When the glue dries, drive the fastener in place.

TIGHTENING LOOSE JOINTS

Sometimes furniture joints, such as mortise and tenon and doweled joints, come loose through stress. There is no way to repair the joint with fasteners. A nail or screw driven into a joint will violate the looks of a piece and, in all likelihood cause real damage. A mortise and tenon or a dowel joint consists of parts cut to fit together snugly. They are glued; no other fastener is used. Chair rungs and legs are typical examples of this type of joint.

Regluing Joints

This repair is relatively simple: take the loose joint completely apart, scrape off the old glue, apply fresh glue, and put the parts back together. Clamp the joint securely until the glue sets. This sounds simple but, unfortunately, taking one joint apart can create stress on other joints, loosening them enough so that you will then need to fix all the joints. You will have to work carefully.

Use a soft mallet or hammer with a soft protective pad of some sort to gently tap apart the loose joint. Tap gently so that the joint comes apart without causing you to break or mar anything. Check other joints. If they are loose also, tap them free.

Scrape away old glue, apply fresh glue and clamp the parts together (see instructions below on "Using Clamps"). If the joint is not worn, white glue at

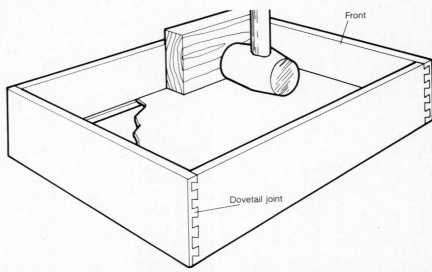

Front

Dovetail joint

Whenever taking a fitted joint (dowel, mortise and tenon or dovetail) apart, use a protective block and a wooden or rubber mallet to separate the parts without damage.

full strength normally can be used with very good success. Immediately wipe away any glue that oozes out of the joint.

Using a Glue Gun for Enlarged Sockets

If you find that there is a gap in the joint because pressure has enlarged

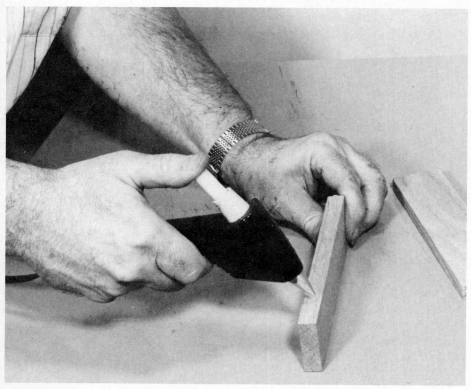

A glue gun may be used to resecure dowel/socket joints if the sections are still quite snug. The glue will fill the small gaps and hold the parts securely together.

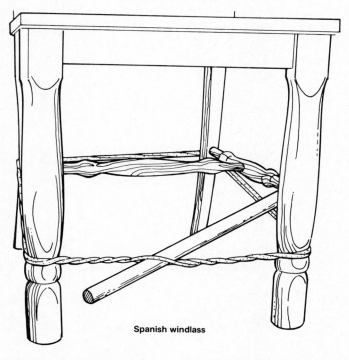

Spanish windlass

If you have resecured chair stretchers with glue, use a Spanish windlass to hold the unit firmly until the glue has set. All you need is soft rope and a dowel.

the socket or the wood has dried and shrunk with age, white glue probably will not be enough to make the joint secure. To compensate for the variance in size, you can add thin pieces of wood to the outside of the end of the rung or in the leg socket to make the joint fit snug. You also may use a filling type of glue. One such is Casein. An excellent and easy to use glue/filler of fairly recent vintage is hot-melt glue. This glue is extruded by an inexpensive ''gun''; the glue fills and holds at the same time. Solid glue sticks are inserted in the back of the gun and heated in a chamber to the hot-melt state. Depending upon the model, the material is extruded by pressing a trigger or pushing the glue stick into the chamber.

If you use hot-melt glue, hold the joint together for thirty seconds to a minute. No clamping is required. If you use other glues, clamping is required.

Using a Spanish Windlass There are many clamps that you can buy, but you can also make your own from a length of cord and a stick. The device is known as a ''Spanish windlass''. To use this, wrap the cord around the parts to be clamped. Twist the stick in the cord, then turn the stick until full pressure is applied by the cord to the joint, then position the stick so the cord cannot come loose. The Spanish windlass is an excellent clamping device for chair legs and rungs.

It is advisable to insert a rag under the cord at each point it comes in contact with the wood so there is no chance for the cord to cause a blemish.

Using Bar Clamps

Bar clamps are available from rental stores and may be purchased in hardware and building supply stores that have special sections for furniture builders. Bar clamps come in many sizes; some are even large enough to clamp a chest of drawers or a full-size bed headboard.

Bar clamps are good for holding sections of furniture in square and for holding boards being edge glued. You must place pieces of soft wood between the wood being clamped and the faces of the jaws holding the wood. You must also be sure that the clamps are attached so that the jaws are flat. If you apply uneven pressure, the clamps will not hold the piece being glued in square. To place the bar clamps, open the jaws wider than the piece you will be clamping and then, depending on the size of the piece and the clamps, slip the clamps or the piece in place. Close the jaws slowly and tighten evenly. Check for perfect square and adjust as needed.

Wedge Clamps

If you cannot find bar clamps, you can make an effective clamp quite inexpensively. Use a piece of 2x4 stock about one foot longer than the piece you wish to clamp. Nail 4x4 inch sections of ¾ inch plywood to the 2x4, spacing the blocks 3 inches farther apart than the full width of the piece to be clamped. Cut another piece of ¾ inch plywood 4 inches by 6 inches. Cut the 4 by 6 inch piece of plywood

diagonally to make two wedge-shape pieces.

To clamp, place the piece between the two blocks and slip one wedge against the piece so that the long, thin, flat face of the wedge is against the piece being clamped. Fit the second wedge in place and gently tap each wedge successively so that the wedges force the piece being clamped against one block. The wedges, of course, are securely placed between the second block and the piece being clamped. Check for square and support the other end of the piece being clamped so the section is level.

This type of clamp may be adjusted for size and used over and over. If you are clamping several sections of furniture or several drawers, you can make any number of wedge clamps at very little cost.

Installing a Spline in Very Loose Joints

Sometimes a socket can enlarge or the end of a rung or a leg can wear

so badly that filling the joint is not enough. In this case you may be able to insert a spline (a thin wedge of wood) in the end of the rung or the leg to widen it so that the rung or leg fills the socket better.

To do this, use a saw to make a cut ¾ inch deep in the end of the rung or the leg. Cut a small wedge of wood, slightly larger than the saw cut, and tap it into the cut in the end of the piece. As you do this, the wedge will expand the end of the rung or leg so that once it is glued in place, the rung or leg will stay firmly in the socket.

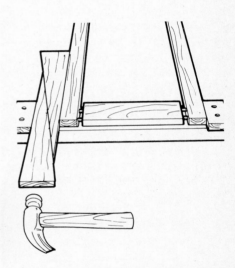

A wedge clamp can be made to size for almost any project that can be laid flat. The wedges force the joints firmly closed.

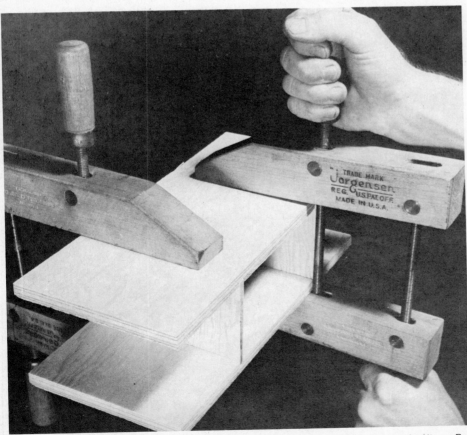

These screw clamps are one of the type of clamps available for use in repairing furniture. Bar clamps, long rods with movable braces, can be used on the largest pieces.

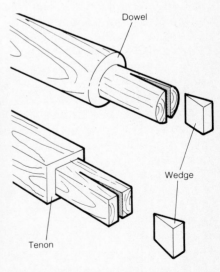

If the dowel or tenon section has shrunk or worn, a small wedge set into a cut in the end will make it fit into the socket firmly.

FIXING WOBBLY FURNITURE

Tables may wobble because one, or more, of the legs is loose. However, there are various other reasons for this problem—and various solutions.

A chest of drawers can be wobbly for the same reasons as a table. In addition, the floor may be uneven or one side or one leg of the chest may be shorter than another(s).

LEVELING A SHORT TABLE LEG

First, shift the table to another location. Perhaps it wobbles because the floor is uneven and one leg is not making complete contact. However, it may be that the wobble is caused by one leg being shorter than another. Put a level on the top of the table and adjust the table until the bubble is centered, then get down to see if there is a gap beneath the floor and leg. If there is, cut a patch of wood the same thickness as the gap and secure the patch to the bottom of the leg with white glue.

If the legs are loose, check the fit of the socket joints or tighten all bolts or screws that hold the legs. Repair joints if loose or worn.

LEVELING A CHEST OF DRAWERS

If the chest is sitting on an uneven floor or if one side or leg is short, this may make the chest seem wobbly. It will also distort the shape of the chest and may cause the drawers to rub and ride unevenly inside their compartments. Before doing anything else, move the dresser to a new spot. If the problem was created by an uneven floor, this may straighten the chest. With the chest in square, the drawers should work freely again.

If this does not solve the problem, then one side could be lower than the other. To correct this, glue a shim to the side of the dresser than is shorter than the other. Use a spirit level to check, but if the drawers work smoothly, it is likely that the chest is level.

REPAIRING STICKING DRAWERS

A chest or cabinet may have drawers that are hard to open or close. There are a variety of possible causes. All problems should, of course, be cor-

rected before any refinishing work is done. Sometimes a drawer will slide into its compartment nicely until the last inch or so. This means that the bottom edges of the drawer are worn except for this last inch, and this causes the drawer the stick. To solve this problem, you may simply press thumbtacks into the bottom edges on which the drawer rides. This will raise the drawer enough so that it will close tightly. The thumbtacks will not be too thick.

You may find that a drawer sticks because it has gotten out of square. Remove the drawer from the chest and check. If it is out of square, you should be able to take it apart easily because the fasteners and/or glue are no longer holding the parts securely. Scrape away the old glue and reglue the drawer and clamp it securely, using one of the methods described above. Check the drawer for square

before allowing the glue to set.

Be sure that all drawer guides are smooth. Replace worn or broken guides.

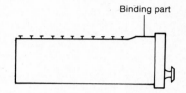

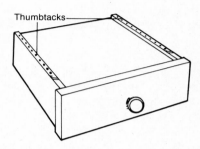

When an old drawer has worn down the side rails, you may install a line of thumbtacks to raise the worn section level with the front.

Bar clamps can be used to secure a new or remade drawer into square while the glue dries.

If glue does not seem to hold a drawer, you may attach parts with fine finishing nails.

4

Removing Old Finishes, Preparing for New

If your piece of furniture or woodwork already has a finish on it, there are several ways to change the finish. Probably the most common and satisfying means of handling the job is to remove the existing finish and to apply a new finish.

First, you must determine that an old finish should be removed. The criteria we apply are simple: Does the wood under the current finish look good? Is the piece not hopelessly dented: Will a new finish repair or hide existing mars? If the answers are "yes," then the piece is a candidate for refinishing. Remove the old finish and apply a new one.

FINISH REMOVAL OPTIONS

There are five common choices for removing a finish from wood: application of heat or flame, sanding, use of a commercial service hot bath or spray stripper, professional hand stripping or stripping the finish by hand yourself.

Heat/Flame

Two common techniques for removal of a finish, especially paint, are use of a blowtorch or a heat gun. Using a blowtorch is always risky. The flame may scorch or ignite the wood. If you do choose this method, reserve it for exterior work. There are several heater/removers on the market, but these are usually effective only as paint removers. They are meant primarily for removal of paint on interior woodwork and are especially useful in removing paint for woodwork in older homes.

Sanding

Removing a finish by sanding it off usually is not a good idea. You risk removing part of the wood along with the finish, because the sand paper may cut through the finish unevenly. For example, if you use a belt sander to remove a painted finish, you might apply just a little too much pressure in one spot and dish the area.

In some cases, sandpaper may be used to remove a finish, but care must be taken or too much wood may be worn away in one spot.

The only place where sanding may be useful—at least in the opinion of this author—is on a piece in particularly bad condition, covered with many layers of thick paint or with a gouged finish. Of course, machine sanding is useful for smoothing wood; the tools and techniques are detailed in Chapter 2.

Commercial Stripping

If a piece is thickly coated with paint, you may want to have the wood commercially stripped by a vat bath or spray method. One central caution should be kept in mind when considering commercial stripping: commercial stripping

The most obvious method of stripping a finish is with a chemical compound. An old finish is removed rapidly; the original wood revealed.

A heat gun softens paint or varnish. This tool is best for removing finishes on woodwork. It is safe for removing lead-base paint.

can cause damage. Do not have a piece commercially stripped if that piece is delicate. Never commercially strip a piece of furniture that has veneer or small, thin parts. A commercial stripper may attack glue in joints, deaden the wood—take the patina from it—or raise the grain. Also, the method is costly; stripping some larger pieces of furniture may cost as much as $75.00 or more.

Hot Bath One professionally employed method for removing a finish is an immersion system. The furniture piece is submerged in a heated caustic solution for twenty minutes or more to remove most or all of the finish. Very little additional work is required to remove the rest. The caustic solution is usually lye heated to 140° and is unsuitable for many pieces of furniture. However, this system does work very effectively on items like shutters, solid doors and metal objects that will be painted. Wood stripped with this method may be bleached to a grey.

Hosing Another technique is the hosing method. A piece is positioned in a tank and an operator sprays remover with a hose. The remover is recirculated and reused. This system is safer than immersion, but it is still difficult to guarantee that the work will be a total success. Remove delicate sections and pieces with thin veneers before you have a unit hosed down.

Professional Hand Finishing

The final professional method of stripping, safe but time-consuming and expensive, is by hand. This is the same technique the do-it-yourselfer uses, but professional wood strippers use stronger chemicals than are available to do-it-yourselfers. If you really want to have a professional strip your furniture, visit a number of refinishers. If you live in a large city, look under Furniture Refinishing in the Yellow Pages to find a listing of professionals. Before making a choice, ask to see samples of their

work—pieces that are going back to their customers. The wood surface should not look waxy or have any old finish on it; the wood should not look pulpy, which would mean that the grain has been raised; nor should the surface appear "dead". Be sure that they will handle your piece with care, and that all work is guaranteed.

MATERIALS FOR DOING IT YOURSELF

There are several materials that can be used to remove a finish from wood. Lacquer thinner takes off lacquer; denatured alcohol removes shellac. However, refinishing usually requires your dealing with chemical compounds designed to remove paint and varnish from furniture or other wood surfaces in your home.

Paint and Varnish Removers

These removers come as liquid, semipaste, and paste. The consistency ranges from jellied material to a thin liquid. The liquid type remover is meant for use on horizontal surfaces only—it will run right off vertical surfaces, and it makes little sense to consider its use when a semi-paste will serve better.

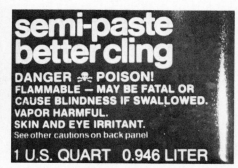

Semi-paste is one type of stripper. The thicker the stripper the more closely it will adhere to the finish. Read directions carefully.

Removers are classified as water washoff, solvent washoff, or no wash. This means that after the remover has been applied and the loosened finish has been scraped off, the residue either must be washed off with water, with a solvent, or need not be removed. It is advisable to clean the surface of all remover before starting any refinishing steps.

Water Soluble Remover The water washoff remover contains detergents that allow the remover to be rinsed off with water. Remember, however, that water and wood—particularly delicate veneers—do not mix well. Water in any

When properly applied and allowed to work, chemical stripper will lift a finish off the wood so that it can be scraped away with a dull-edge, flexible tool such as this one.

quantity can attack the structural integrity of a piece of furniture and raise the wood grain on any wood, requiring additional steps when refinishing.

Solvent Wash Removers Some paint and varnish removers must be rinsed from the surface with a solvent. The solvent, often denatured alcohol or a petroleum distillate, is usually applied with a rag and rubbed with steel wool.

Cautions and Recommendations In addition to the categories listed above, removers also can be divided into regular removers and those designed for surfaces on which silicone polishes have been used. Silicones impregnate the wood fibers and can prevent the wood from accepting a new finish. Attempting to apply a new finish to an apparently clean surface filled with silicone wax will create a surface with pinpoint spots or craters and fisheyes where the silicone residue has rejected the new finish. No-wax type removers designed to remove silicones are preferred as long as use is followed by a good, final cleaning.

Removing silicone from wood To clean furniture that has been polished with silicone products, use a cloth dampened with turpentine and sprinkled with powdered laundry detergent. Rub the surface of the wood in the direction of the grain to wash the finish. Change cloths frequently to prevent the dirt and silicones from being redeposited on the finish.

Rinse the finish clean with fresh turpentine to remove all traces of detergent. Do this before and after applying the stripper to be sure all silicone has been removed.

Removers, like other products, vary in their formulas and in effectiveness in different situations, so there is always a question of which is best for your job. Some removers evaporate faster than others; this means you will spend more time and use more material to complete the job. Some removers are expensive, and some simply are not as effective as others. There are many excellent removers available, and this author has used several that he has found consistently effective, among them Bix, Zar and Strypeeze. These are widely available, but there are other fine products available. In any case, ask for advice before making your purchase, describing your refinishing project so the salesperson knows your requirements. You may also want to buy a small container of remover to try on a scrap or an unobtrusive area. This will test the product's effectiveness and help you develop your removal skills.

Warning: Precautions It must be noted that there are no effective cleaning solvents available that are completely hazard-free. Some strippers and solvents are flammable, others are toxic. Read the label precautions and follow all directions. Do not breathe fumes; do not allow solvents to contact the skin. Do not use solvents and strippers near a flame. Never use a stripper or any solvent in a room with a gas appliance. Do not smoke or allow smoking near solvents or strippers. Prolonged exposure to certain fumes may precipitate a cardiac irregularity.

The best place to strip wood is on a covered porch or patio. If you must work indoors—when stripping woodwork, for instance—always work with the windows open and have an exhaust fan in one window. If it is too cold or rainy to keep the windows open, do not do finish removal work.

Silicone polishes enter wood through scratches and make the surface impervious to stain. Silicones must be removed before refinishing.

Rub a paste of turpentine and detergent on the wood before and after stripping to remove the silicone residue for good refinishing.

STRIPPING OFF THE OLD FINISH

Before starting to strip any piece of furniture, remove all hardware, upholstery or caning, if possible. If the metal hardware has been painted and you want to remove this finish from it, drop the hardware in a container filled with remover. The longer the hardware soaks, the easier it will be to remove the paint.

Wherever possible remove all hardware and other metal trim from furniture before stripping the finish. Label pieces and store safely.

Work Procedures

It is, of course, imperative to follow specific label instructions for all products used; however, the following basic steps should explain the typical application and use of paint and varnish removers.

Step 1: Preparing the Work Area Protect all floors and surrounding areas with newspapers. Apply remover to one area at a time. If a piece is very small, you may apply remover to the entire piece. Apply the remover carefully so that it does not drip on an area where you do not want the finish removed, or drip from one area onto another. The remover can create spot marks on the surface if the volatile spirits evaporate and the residue hardens. Use newspaper held with masking tape to protect parts to be treated later. If the newspaper becomes damp from the stripper, replace it. If you do not want to be bothered with using newspaper, you will have to watch your work carefully and wipe off any dripped or spattered remover immediately.

Step 2: Applying the Stripper Use a brush and apply the remover thickly, spreading it only in one direction. Allow time for the stripper to work; the manufacturer's directions will include

Stripper is usually best applied with a brush. Pour some stripper into a convenient container that will not be damaged by the chemical. Action usually begins immediately.

The stripper and finish may be scraped off with a flat tool. If the finish is not thick, steel wool will clean and smooth the surface. Change steel wool or clean your tools frequently.

information on reasonable "standing time" for the stripper to do most lifting. The single most common sin of do-it-yourself refinishers is not allowing the remover to remain in place long enough to work completely. In this case, an anxious or eager stripper may double his work and his working time. The time required for the stripper to work will vary according to the weather. In hot weather finish removers evaporate quickly; you may have to apply additional coats. If you are working out of doors, always work in the shade. Depending on the weather and the temperature, you may have

to leave the remover on the surface for an hour or more. The function of the remover is to lift the surface finish; it should do the work, not you. When the finish begins to look crinkly, or when you can expose wood by rubbing the surface with steel wool, the finish is ready to be scraped off.

Step 3: Scraping off the Stripper To remove the stripper and the finish without damaging the wood, use as wide and as smooth a scraper as you can. Use a scraper with rounded corners, such as a joint compound knife. Use steel wool to remove any finish embedded in the wood grain. Scrape

The stripper raises the finish and liquifies part of the material. Allow stripper to work as long as directed for full effect.

If the stripper has been allowed to work properly, the finish should scrape off with little resistance and leave a minimum residue.

The softened finish may become quite spongy and sticky. You will probably have to clean the scraper often. Exposed wood shows scratches that extended through the finish.

all the material off. When the surface is clean, use the washing solution recommended by the manufacturer to clean the stripper off the surface.

Stripping carved or turned wood

At some point in stripping furniture, and, in many cases, woodwork, you probably will have to remove finish from grooves and carving. To do this, use a probing tool—an orange stick, dowel sharpened to a point, old toothbrush or wood skewer—to scrape stripper from grooves and curves. The ends of these tools are relatively soft and should not scratch the wood. To clear grooves in legs and rungs, braid

Steel wool can be used to lift finish and stripper out of grooves and turnings. Rub the length of steel wool across the turned area.

To give steel wool more strength, especially when using thin sections to clean out fine turnings, twist the steel wool around twine.

Protect your hands when using stripper. Although some strippers are more irritating than others, all are toxic and can cause reactions on the skin and irritation to lungs and heart.

a length of 00 steel wool into a rope. Pull it back and forth in the grooves with a ''shoeshine'' action. This fine grade of steel wool polishes and smoothes the wood.

After the first coat of stripper has been removed, you may find there are areas that still retain some of the finish. This means you must apply a second coat of remover. Do this in exactly the same way you applied the first: brush it on in one direction, thickly, and let it set. Then scrape and wash as directed.

Controlling evaporation On very hot days, remover can evaporate quickly. To prevent this, apply the remover to the surface, then cover the piece with a plastic drop cloth to retard evaporation. You may find that you can leave the remover on for hours-–even overnight, but check the progress of evaporation regularly. Do not let the remover become totally dry.

It may mar the natural color of the wood. Dried remover cannot be scraped off. If the remover does dry, apply a fresh coat to soften and reactivate the dried remover. Then scrape the surface. If necessary, use a third coat of remover.

Step 4: Cleaning the Surface After all the finish has been removed, give the wood the required bath to clean off and neutralize any residue from the remover.

If you have used a water-wash remover, use 00 steel wool and water to remove the residue. Dip the steel wool in the water, squeeze out the excess and then stroke the steel wool across the surface in the direction of the grain. If you used a solvent or even a no-wash, you can use a wash of denatured alcohol. This also is applied with steel wool. Follow the denatured alcohol application by rubbing the surface with a paint thinner such as Var-

noline. Use a natural bristle brush to remove residue from turnings and carvings. Some product instructions do not mention residue cleanup or suggest it is not necessary, but experience has shown that it is always advisable to clear surface of any residue of stripper.

Re-using Remover
It is possible to reuse remover under certain conditions. Remover used for a second or third application to vertical surfaces will be relatively clean. Use a small can to collect the remover as it runs down the surface. If you are using a paste remover, you should be able to scrape the relatively clean remover into a container to be used elsewhere on the project. The stripper will retain most of its strength if kept in a tightly sealed jar.

USING SOLVENTS ON SHELLAC OR LACQUER

Paint and varnish removers will take off paint, epoxy, varnish, shellac and synthetic finishes no matter how thickly they were put on. The process is, of course, messy. If the finish to be removed is shellac or lacquer, it is easier and less messy to strip these materials with solvents that are part of the lacquer or shellac formulation.

Identifying the Finish
New furniture with a hard, high gloss finish is usually coated with lacquer. To test the finish, dab an out-of-the-way spot with a soft rag to which you have applied lacquer thinner. If the finish clouds but regains its gloss when the lacquer thinner has evaporated, the finish is lacquer.

Denatured alcohol will dissolve shellac. Apply denatured alcohol to a rag and dab it on a hidden spot on the surface. If the finish shows on the rag or liquifies, the finish is shellac.

If you dab lacquer thinner on varnish, the surface will crinkle, which may lead you to think that the varnish is lacquer. If the surface remains crinkled, the finish is varnish. To remove varnish, you must use one of the paint and varnish strippers. No other solvent will work.

Using Solvent on Shellac
Work in a well-ventilated room or out of doors when removing shellac with denatured alcohol. You will need steel wool and several clean soft rags. Pour a small amount of alcohol on the surface, rub the area with the steel wool, and wipe off the residue with rags. Work on only a small section at a time.

You may find the shellac resistant to the alcohol. This usually indicates

You may apply the denatured alcohol with steel wool. This will apply the alcohol and remove the finish in one action.

To remove shellac from turnings, apply the denatured alcohol with an old toothbrush. Use the brush to clean the finish from the area.

that the shellac has had a little lacquer added to it. To remove a combination finish like this, add a little lacquer thinner to the alcohol. Follow removal technique described for alcohol.

Using Solvent on Lacquer
Apply lacquer thinner to the lacquered finish in the same manner you applied alcohol to the shellacked finish. You may find the process easier if you add a little, but just a little, denatured alcohol to the lacquer thinner. Reverse the proportions of alcohol and thinner given for removing shellac with solvent, and follow the same steps in order to remove the lacquer.

Removing Alternating Layers of Shellac and Lacquer
If you find a finish that seems not to react to either alcohol or thinner, the finish could consist of alternate coats of lacquer and shellac. To remove this combination, mix alcohol and thinner half and half, and apply the mixture with steel wool. If this formula works, remove the finish with steel wool and clean rags as described above.

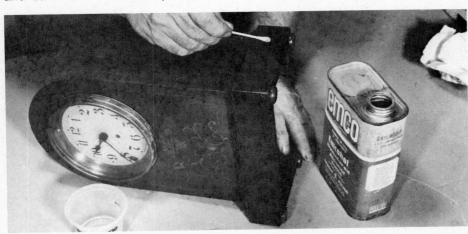
Older pieces may have a shellac finish. Soak a cotton swab in denatured alcohol and rub the swab across the finish. Do this is an inconspicuous area to avoid marring the surface.

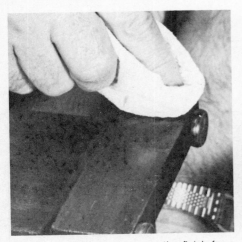
After the alcohol has been on the finish for a short time, the surface should soften. Rub the area to which you have applied alcohol.

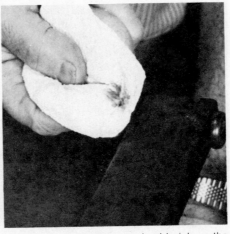
If the finish is shellac, you should pick up the softened finish on a clean rag. You may then use alcohol to remove the finish.

PREPARING THE SURFACE FOR REFINISHING

After all the old finish has been removed from any wood, the surface should be prepared for the new finish. Check for problem areas and discolorations where the stripper was not completely removed.

Oil and Grease

Oil and grease frequently penetrate the finish on wood and are absorbed into the wood fibers. This grease and oil must be removed or a new finish will not adhere to the wood.

Solvent Treatment Set the wood out of doors or in a very well-ventilated area and scrub the surface with a dry cleaning solvent. Wear rubber gloves and, if possible, a respirator. Use a brush to apply the solvent. Rub with 000 steel wool. Allow the wood to dry thoroughly. Repeat the treatment two or three times, allowing the wood to dry a day between treatments. If white specks appear after you apply the dry cleaning solvent, then food once dried on the surface. Repeat the treatment

as often as needed until the surface is clean.

Absorbent Treatment If the surface was regularly in contact with oil or greasy materials, the wood should be given a special treatment.

Make a paste of fuller's earth (an absorbent powder available at paint stores) and dry cleaning solvent. Apply the paste to the surface of the wood and leave it on for 24 hours. The solvent will dissolve the grease, which will then be absorbed by the fuller's earth. When the paste is dry, brush it off. Repeat treatment until the surface is clear of grease and then treat the wood with straight solvent.

Smooth the surface with 120 or 240 garnet paper.

If you are sanding a flat surface, wrap the abrasive around a block, or an electric in-line sander. (See Chapter Two for directions on making a sanding block.) For curved items, wrap the sandpaper around a rubber ball. When the sanding has been com-

pleted, wipe off the dust with a dusting brush. Follow this by wiping with a tack rag.

Dark Spots

The most common means of removing stains from bare wood calls for mild bleach. Bleach also may be used to freshen wood color if it has become gray or faded. Maple, for example, becomes gray as it ages.

Oxalic Acid Crystal Bleach To make the wood bleach, put 2 ounces (about 4 level tablespoonfuls) of oxalic acid crystals (available at paint and hardware stores) and 2 ounces of tartaric acid powder (available at drugstores and chemical supply houses) in a half-gallon, heat-resistant glass or enamel container. Pour a quart of hot water over the crystals to dissolve them.

Apply the solution (while hot) to the stained wood with a small cloth. Keep the surface wet. Turn and change the cloths frequently as you apply the so-

Unfinished or stripped wood may be marred by grease or oil. Clean away these spots before any refinishing material is applied.

To clean grease from wood, saturate the spot with dry cleaning fluid and cover the area with fuller's earth to absorb the grease.

lution. Allow the bleach to remain on the wood for about 20 minutes.

After the dark spot has lightened, you should neutralize the bleach that remains on the surface so it does not damage the wood. Add one tablespoonful of clear, not sudsy, ammonia to one quart cold water. Wash off the bleach with the ammonia solution. Dip clean cloths in clear water, squeeze, and wipe the surface. Wipe again, this time with dry cloths, and let dry 24 hours.

If the dark spots have not disappeared within 24 hours, repeat bleach application and drying process. After you have used this bleaching solution, be sure to wear a mask during the sanding and smoothing process.

Oxalic acid will also remove old water and ink stains.

Oxalic Acid Substitutes Oxalic acid crystals are no longer available in some areas. If you cannot find oxalic acid crystals, choose from one of these options.

There are some products marketed as substitutes for oxalic acid. Ask your local hardware seller for suggestions. If you find one of these substitutes, use 2 ounces of the substitute and 2 ounces of tartaric acid in 1 quart of hot water. You can neutralize with full strength, 5 percent acetic acid (white vinegar). This solution is the most effect bleach on maple. Allow wood to dry outdoors or indoors with good air circulation.

Other Bleaches Another bleach substitute is a mixture of one tablespoonful of household ammonia (clear) and one quart of water. If you use sudsy ammonia, rinse the surface with clear water and then dry it.

A less acceptable choice is full strength denatured alcohol solvent applied with 000 steel wool. Use a natural fiber brush to apply to carvings and turnings.

The last choice is commercial stain remover or chlorine bleach. When using chlorine bleach, use a solution twice as strong as suggested for fabric. Allow the bleach to dry on the wood. Rinse and let dry in the shade.

There are wood bleaching kits available. Discuss this with your dealer.

Observe all precautions for safe handling of all removers, solvents and bleach. Protect all working-area surfaces from accidental contact with these materials. Check carefully before mixing any chemicals. Although ammonia serves as a neutralizer for oxalic acid, it must never be combined with chlorine.

Apply wood bleach to dark spots that may be left after you have used stripper. The bleach will make the wood more even in tone.

Work the bleach into the wood and let it stand long enough to be effective. Check action by rubbing a little of the bleach off.

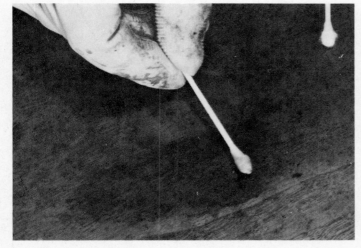

Neutralize the bleach to prevent overbleaching and damage to the wood. Allow the wood to dry thoroughly before attempting to refinish.

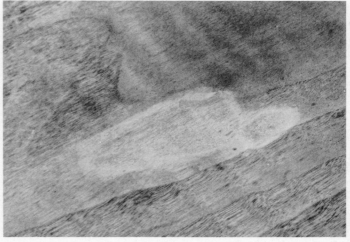

The area that has been bleached is noticeable but is similar in tone to the rest of the wood and will match when the wood is refinished.

5

Finishes and Refinishing

When the wood is bare and clean, has been sanded well, patched and repaired, and stains removed as required, then it is ready for finishing. This is the part of the finishing or renewal process that people seem to enjoy most.

CHOOSING THE STAIN

There is a wide variety of ways that wood can be finished. Application of a stain is the basic first step. Staining is done to improve the appearance of wood unless the natural color and grain is already very handsome. Stain can give wood the color and appearance you want. It gives dissimilar woods a more uniform appearance and adds a lively color to old wood that has faded or lost its color in stripping. Stain does not protect the wood from damage or moisture, so application of stain is generally followed with a final finish of oil, shellac, lacquer or varnish.

Should You Use Stain?

In many instances you will have no doubt that a piece of wood should be stained. At other times you may think that just a clear finish is the best choice. To help you decide, keep in mind how the wood looked while it was damp during refinishing. If you are finishing a new piece, or if you cannot recall the color difference, wet part of the wood with water. The "wet look" will approximate how the wood would look with a clear finish. If you like this look, do not stain the wood.

What and When to Stain

Although you will be finishing the wood to suit your personal taste, before you start you should be aware of basic and

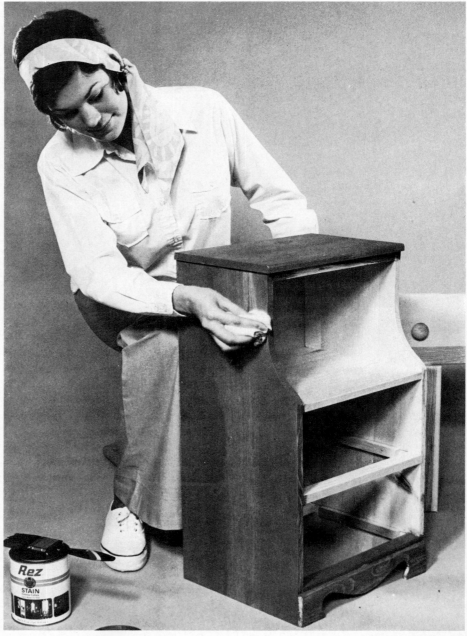

Staining is usually the first step in refinishing a piece of furniture. The stain will enhance or change the natural color of the wood and allow you to control the final finished look.

accepted practices related to wood and stain combinations.

Woods that usually are not stained because of their inherent beauty and color are: butternut, cherry, mahogany, maple, myrtle, rosewood, teak and walnut.

In addition, there exists a whole range of woods that are finished with a clear finish under some circumstances and are stained under other circumstances. In these cases, the decision to stain or not is usually based solely on personal taste. The woods in this category include: ash, beech, birch, chestnut, elm, maple, oak, mahogany (Philippine type).

Effects of Staining

Different woods will absorb stain differently, depending on the relative hardness or softness of the wood. Woods that are hard, such as maple, birch and oak, do not take stain as easily because it cannot penetrate or be absorbed readily. Physically soft woods, such as poplar, pine or basswood, absorb stain quickly and absorb it in greater quantities.

No matter how hard the wood is physically, it can be stained well. However, other factors also influence the manner and degree in which the wood absorbs stain. One factor is the coarseness of the wood. A coarse-surfaced wood will absorb more stain than a smooth-finished surface; that is, one that has been carefully sanded.

Another factor is the stain itself. Some stains penetrate more deeply into the wood than others.

The most important factor, however, is the way the stain is applied and how long it remains on the surface. If the stain is applied and then allowed to remain for some time on the surface, it will penetrate more deeply than if it were applied and wiped off quickly.

Testing the Stain To test how a stain will look, apply stain to the underside of a piece. This process will help you see the potential result. When testing stain, and even when coating the entire piece, it is a good idea to do the work in strong natural light. Only natural light will give you a true impression of the color. Incandescent and fluorescent light can change the appearance of the stain color drastically.

Lightening the Stain If you make a mistake, it is possible, by wiping off the

Cherry is one wood that is often left unstained. The lightly stained section at the right shows the grain intensified. Darker stain, shown at the left, hides the grain.

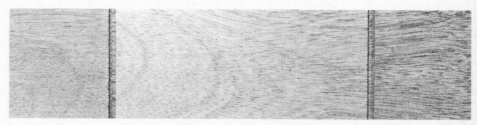

Some woods, such as Honduras mahogany, show little change in the grain pattern whether stained dark or light. You may start with a light stain and add more in a second application.

Ash has a strong grain pattern. In the case of this wood, you may want to use stain to make the grain seem less noticeable and blend into the overall tone of the finish.

When you are dealing with delicate grain with little contrast, use care in choosing the stain or the color may cover the grain entirely as shown here on the left.

With a wood such as Ponderosa pine, shown here, application of a stain may change the appearance and color to approximate other wood as well as to heighten natural grain.

A light stain will sharply intensify the grain on some wood, such as red oak, and make a dramatic difference in the appearance. A dark stain hides this grain.

stain with solvent or by sanding the area, to lighten spots that have absorbed too much stain. (These steps will be covered in more detail later in this chapter.) The end grain, which is more porous than the flat, top grain, will absorb more stain. Unless you want the end grain to appear darker than the surface of the wood, dilute the stain. Use whatever is specified on the container to dilute the solution.

Birch is often stained to match other woods. A dark stain creates an almost solid finish. A light stain gives depth and interest to the surface pattern.

Practice staining and wiping off stain before doing the finished piece. Here, wet stain is wiped away to lighten the effect.

Types of Stain

There are a number of different types of stain available, and they will all serve your purposes. There is water stain, latex stain, penetrating oil stain (also known as wiping stain), lacquer stain, alcohol stain, and its close cousin NGR stains. Each is useful, but their individual effectiveness varies in different situations.

Water stain This stain comes in a variety of colors such as red, yellow and blue as well as wood colors. You buy it as a powder and add water to make the stain. The more water you add, the more the material is diluted and the lighter the stain becomes. Conversely, the more powder you add, the bolder or strong the color becomes.

Wiping Stain If the different sections of wood are really dissimilar in appearance, a wiping oil stain should be used. Wiping oil has the capacity to even out the looks of the wood. The material is thick and is also a good pore filler. Wiping oil is available in a variety of wood colors.

Alcohol Stain A number of companies make a stain with an alcohol base.

These products can be very useful, but they must be applied carefully. They dry very fast and on long surfaces they may dry to a streaky, splotchy finish. However, because the alcohol stain dries so rapidly, it does not raise the grain of wood as other stains can. Since it is advisable to follow the practice of most finishers and sand any piece after staining, this nongrain-raising advantage is not very important.

If you use an alcohol stain, practice on scrap wood to ensure that a technique good enough for successful application to the piece being finished. If you do encounter problems, most can be corrected.

Lacquer Stain

This material is very similar to alcohol stain. The advantage of this stain is that it dries more slowly than the alcohol stain. The drying time is still relatively short, approximately one hour, but the slower drying does mean that you will have less difficulty with uneven color.

NGR Stains

NGR, or nongrain-raising stain is a close cousin of the alcohol stain. This formulation, which dries quickly before the moisture can raise the grain, is favored by professional finishers. The stain comes in a concentrated form that is mixed with a thinner—usually denatured alcohol. The only real difference between NGR and alcohol stain is a slight difference in their formula. However, NGR stains should really be applied with a spray apparatus that takes some experience to master. If you try to apply NGR stain with a brush, the results are likely to be spotty because the stain simply dries too quickly for smooth, even application. It is the kind of stain that you should experiment with before trying it on a good piece of wood.

APPLYING STAIN AND FILLER

When you are filling open-pore wood or repairing minor scratches in the surface of the wood, you will do the filling either before or after the application of the stain. The choice is dependent upon the makeup of the two materials. Some fillers and stains will combine badly unless applied in a certain sequence.

Application directions will appear on the packages. The directions will be specific about the sequence of application. As a guideline, however, remember the following: most fillers will be dissolved by the solvent in alcohol stain. If you are using an alcohol stain, use the stain first and then apply the filler. If you are using a water-base stain, fill the wood before you stain.

Filler that is left on the surface of the wood (not actually filling pores or scratches) may inhibit the absorption of the stain by the wood. The surface should be carefully wiped clean before staining.

Filler that is applied after the wood has been stained must be "dyed to match" the finish of the wood. Filler is sold in either a white or cream color and it will accept color. There is a stain (dye) sold that is specifically formulated to color the filler.

CLEAR FINISHES

In addition to stains, there are clear finishes that you will want to consider for finishing wood. The most common procedure, when finishing or refinishing any wood, is to apply a clear finish as protection because the stain itself, as mentioned, does not provide a protective coat. Clear finishes may be used on unstained wood, but this usually is limited to woods that are naturally attractive.

The standard clear finishes are shellac, varnish, lacquer, polyurethane and oils.

Because shellac is available in many weights, be sure to check to label for the cut you want. You may thin shellac as required.

Shellac

Shellac comes from a material exuded by the Lac beetle, an insect indigenous to South America. The dry exudation is powdered and the powder is then mixed with denatured alcohol. Shellac comes in various cuts. This means that a specified amount of alcohol has been added to a specified amount of shellac flakes. The common denominator is one gallon of denatured alcohol. When one speaks of a five pound cut, one means that five pounds of lac flakes have been dissolved in one gallon of denatured alcohol. A two pound cut would refer to a solution of two pounds of lac flakes dissolved in a gallon of alcohol. The lower the cut number, the more alcohol it contains and the thinner the consistency of the shellac. If you are a beginning woodworker, you probably will find the 2-pound cut easiest to work with. The chart indicates other cuts, and it shows how to convert standard store-bought cuts into various other dilutions or consistencies.

Characteristics of Shellac Shellac comes in two colors, designated white and orange. The orange is actually am-

PROPORTIONS FOR SHELLAC CUTS

Shellac	Alcohol	Resulting Cut
2 parts 5 lb.	1 part	3 lb.
1 part 5 lb.	1 part	2 lb.
1 part 5 lb.	2 parts	1 lb.
1 part 4 lb.	2 parts	3 lb.
4 parts 4 lb.	3 parts	2 lb.
1 part 4 lb.	4 parts	1 lb.
5 parts 3 lb.	2 parts	2 lb.
3 parts 3 lb.	4 parts	1 lb.

ber in color, and the white shellac is cream color. If you wish, you can mix the two colors to create something in between. Of the two, the orange shellac gives a brighter look to woods with yellow orange tones, such as cherry and mahogany.

Shellac works well as a sealer coat and is good for small jobs on surfaces that are not normally subject to moisture, such as lamps, clocks or spice racks. Moisture will cloud shellac and alcohol will soften it, which is why alcohol is used to determine if a piece has a shellacked surface.

Although it is not as durable as varnish, shellac is the finish found on most antique furniture. It is easy to apply.

VARNISH

Many professional refinishers do not like to use varnish because it takes a long time to dry. For a professional, time is money. Varnish may become damaged during the drying; someone may touch the surface and leave a mark or dust may settle on the surface.

However, varnish is durable and waterproof, and it can be used effectively; many finishers recommend it.

Types of Varnish

Varnish comes in various types. Regular varnishes take up to 24 hours to dry and quick-drying varnishes take approximately five hours to dry. This is much slower than shellac, but it is considerably faster than regular varnish.

The composition of varnish differs slightly from type to type, but they all

basically are formulated with natural resins, oil (either tung or linseed) and a solvent or thinner such as turpentine. Polyurethanes, which will be discussed in some detail later, also are classed as varnishes. The essential ingredient in paint—the material that makes it stick and cover—is varnish. Indeed, in the trade, paint is considered a colored varnish.

Varnish is available in various degrees of gloss from flat to high. There is also a formula designated as rubbing varnish. This is formulated so that it can be rubbed with pumice stone and oil to produce a super high gloss. Many finishers like the appearance created when flat finish varnish is used over coats of high gloss varnish.

LACQUERS

Lacquer is the finish most favored by professionals because it quickly produces a hard, durable, good looking finish. It dries almost immediately.

Characteristics of Lacquer

The one big disadvantage of lacquer is actually the same as its major advantage; it dries very rapidly. Lacquer application must be perfect; there is no second chance to go over it and brush out imperfections. Therefore, lacquer is usually applied with a sprayer. This may

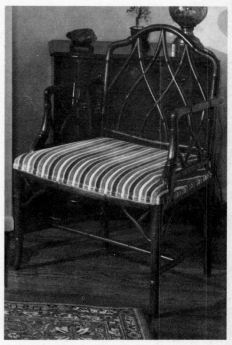

Commercially manufactured furniture has a lacquer finish. This is applied with a special spray system for a smooth, durable finish.

create a problem for the do-it-yourselfer who has never used a spray applicator unit. Because the lacquer spray units are expensive, purchase is not practical; however, the equipment may be rented.

Brush-on lacquers are also available, but these are not as effective as the sprays. The lacquer dries so quickly that brush marks set instantly, and you can not smooth them out. It also is messy, because you must use a lot of lacquer thinner (the solvent for the material) to keep the lacquer usable, and this is expensive.

If your job is small, you can get the best results using a small spray can of lacquer. However, for large jobs it is too expensive to use spray cans. Lacquer comes in a clear finish, but also can be found in a wide variety of colors. A couple of coats of lacquer usually are all that is required, and no sanding or steel-wool rubbing is needed between coats. Always read and follow the manufacturer's specific directions to ensure successful use.

POLYURETHANES

This is another category of clear finish. Polyurethane has a resin base that is a petroleum derivative. Depending on chemical properties, different polyurethanes produce different results or have different working characteristics.

By definition, polyurethanes are varnishes, but no manufacturer seems to call his product a varnish—an idiosyncracy within the industry.

There are three basic types of polyurethanes. Following is a discussion of each to help you understand the distinctions between each so you will have a better idea of what you are buying. However, in most states you will have to ask the dealer to identify the type, because the states do not require that the product's chemical composition be on the label.

Oil-Modified Polyurethanes

Oil-modified polyurethanes are the urethane finishes most commonly found in the stores. These are modified with linseed, soya or safflower oil. Those modified with linseed produce excellent exterior durability; those with soya offer excellent color retention. Safflower oil is not usually used because it does not have the durability of soya or linseed.

Varnish finishes have the advantage of being resistant to wear and largely waterproof. Polyurethanes are more and more common and are useful for many do-it-yourself projects.

There are two chemical varieties of oil-modified polyurethanes; aromatic and aliphatic. These chemical distinctions within the compounds need not concern the do-it-yourselfer, except that the aromatic are more common because the aliphatic are so expensive to produce. Aliphatic are not as easy to find.

Alkyd Modified

The polyurethanes billed as "alkyd modified" have alkyd resin added to the urethane to produce a finish that has excellent recoatability. Unfortunately, the product has poor durability. Alkyd resins are far less expensive than other urethanes; thus, the less expensive finishes tend to be alkyd modified.

Polyethers

Polyethers are called moisture cure polyurethanes. This group provides outstanding durability, but it is seldom used by do-it-yourselfers because the polyether ingredients are so reactive that they cure in the can unless packaged in a special container that is topped with nitrogen. Even with this special treatment, polyethers have a limited shelf life. Glidden is the only manufacturer of a polyether of which this author is aware.

Catalyzed Polyurethane

Catalyzed is the third category of polyurethane finish. Like an expoy, this must be mixed prior to use. A catalyzed polyurethane gives excellent chemical resistance but has limited shelf life; also it is dangerous to use.

Recommendation to Do-It-Yourselfers

The best choice for the do-it-yourselfer is oil-modified polyurethane. Durability of the urethane varnish is directly related to film thickness; and the more polyurethanes in the mixture, the thicker the film.

FILLERS

In order for clear finishes to be completely effective, open-pore woods must be filled with a paste filler so the surface is smooth. This is particularly important on table and desktops. The filler creates a flat, even surface. When the clear finish is applied, the top will be uninterrupted by grain pattern marks.

OIL FINISHES

Another type of finish you will want to consider is the oil finish. Perhaps the oldest oil finish material is linseed oil. There are two kinds of linseed oil, pure

Woodwork may be an excellent candidate for an oil finish. Fine, old wood will take on a very attractive sheen with oil; however, do not use oil finishes in areas of potential fire.

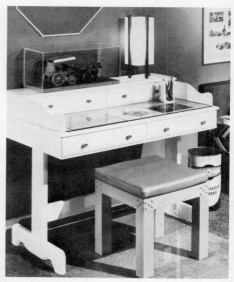

A well-done painted finish can be one of the most attractive alternatives to clear finishes. Paint can add interest to a dull piece.

and boiled. Some linseed oil also has had driers added to the oil. These driers are very important to the wood finishers; without them, the linseed oil would take an impractically long time to dry. So, when buying the oil make sure it says "boiled" and has added driers.

The application of a linseed oil finish requires a lot of elbow grease. Some furniture finishers say that even under the best conditions the process is difficult because the oil requires so much time to dry between coats. On the positive side, the finish is nearly impervious to water and heat, as well as scratches.

PENETRATING OIL

Another type of oil finish is penetrating oil, such as Antique Oil by Minwax, also known in the trade as Danish oil. Like other types of oil, this product is really for use on a beautiful wood, such as teak or walnut. This is the oil finish commonly found on Danish furniture.

Although penetrating oils do give a degree of protection to wood surfaces, they do not provide as much as other clear finishes. On the other hand, penetrating oils are easy to touch up; you do not have to do a complete refinishing to a piece. The penetrating oils impart an attractive, mellow sheen to the wood

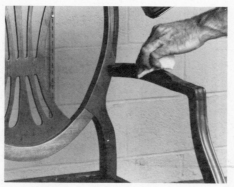

An oil finish is relatively simple to apply, but the process of rubbing in the oil and achieving the polished glow takes time.

and deepen the color. However, if protection is important, linseed oil is better. The advantage of penetrating oil is that it will not build up a film, as will linseed oil. Like other oils, it can be used over stains, and may be applied to any type of wood.

Tung Oil

Another type of available finishing oil is tung oil. Like other oils, it deepens the color of the wood, but does not obscure grain. A good finish requires up to five coats. Each coat adds to the level of gloss. There is a minimum of 36 hours of drying time between coats. Tung oil, like the other finishing oils, penetrates

well into the wood. Its disadvantage is that it is virtually impossible to strip. Most refinishers find that if they need to remove it, the best solution is to sand it off. Therefore, before deciding to use tung oil on a piece of furniture, test the material carefully on a piece of scrap wood.

PAINTING FURNITURE

Although it is usually considered less elegant or less formal, paint serves as a practical finish for many pieces of wood furniture. Paint also is a quick finish. It will go on rapidly and can be applied over any reasonably smooth surface. The paint itself fills in very small pores and scratches.

You can use either latex or oil-base paint for furniture, but the oil-base is preferred. It stands up to wear and tear better than latex and it is available in flat, semi-gloss and high gloss finishes. Latex is available in flat and semi-gloss finishes only. It should be noted that of the two paints, semi- and high-gloss, most people prefer semi-gloss. The appearance is more subdued than the finish of a high-gloss paint, and semi-gloss stands up just as well. Because of the lower reflectivity, surface imperfections and brush marks are not as visible.

Paint is available in a virtually limitless array of colors. Individual manufacturers offer a wide array of off-the-shelf colors and you can always have a color custom-mixed, although this may add a nominal amount to the cost.

USING STAINS

WATER STAIN AND LATEX STAIN
Water stain is simple to use, and it is a good choice to use on interior wood that will be exposed to strong sunlight. It resists fading very well. Water stain also works well on some woods where other stains do not. Cherry and birch, for instance, are difficult to stain because of their dense grain. Other stains often create spots on these woods, but water stain works more evenly on these woods.

Using Water Stain
   Step 1: Mixing the Stain Sprinkle a teaspoonful of powder into a clean quart-size glass jar. Pour a cup of warm water into the jar and mix thoroughly with a stick. Dilute the solution with cold water until the solution reaches the stain color you want. If the color is too weak, you can add more powder for a stronger color. You also can mix in one or two more additional stain powders to create a different color.

   If the water in your area is hard, use distilled water or strain boiled water through several layers of tightly woven nylon cloth, let it cool and reheat it.

   Always test stain on a hidden part of the furniture before doing the entire piece.

   Step 2: Applying the Stain Place the piece you are working on in natural light. Use a wet cloth to dampen the wood. Pay particular attention to turnings and to end grain where absorption is greatest. The application of water will help insure even application or penetration of stain for a richer color.

   Use cheesecloth or other lint-free material to apply the stain. You may use a brush if you prefer. Apply the stain in the direction of the grain. Once a piece is coated, progressively wipe off the stain until you have the color you want. If the color is lighter than you wanted, apply and wipe off another coat of stain.

   Some pieces will be composed of light and dark sections of wood. If you want to obtain a more uniform color, then apply the stain at diluted strength to the darker sections and at a stronger strength to the other. Of course, the

Pour powder for a water stain into a wide-mouth glass jar. This jar will allow you to see the color intensity as you mix the stain.

Add warm water to the powder and mix well. Use distilled water if your tap water is hard to avoid a color shift.

Test stain on the piece of furniture so you will know how the wood will respond to the color. However, use the underside of a chair or the back or a chest or dresser to check color.

Apply the stain with cheesecloth and work along the grain. Test the color intensity frequently so you do not get the stain too dark.

resulting overall tones will vary according to the composition of the wood.

Step 3: Buffing the Wood Allow the piece to dry naturally in an area that has good ventilation. Do not put the piece near a direct heat source because this could cause the wood to dry unevenly and result in a warp.

Allow the piece to dry for twenty-four hours, then buff the surfaces lightly with fine steel wool, grade 000. Take care when buffing the edges of the piece because it is easy to rub the stain off.

WIPING OIL STAIN

The biggest advantage of wiping stain is that it is very easy to apply. Wiping oil stain is wiped on and then it is wiped off until the desired color is achieved. You can apply this stain with a brush or even with paper toweling, if you wish.

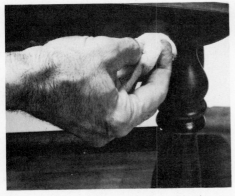

Wiping oil stain is also applied with cheesecloth. Wipe it on and wipe it off until the color is right. Too much will hide the grain.

Different manufacturers recommend different "standing times" before wiping off stain during refinishing. Minwax, for example, advises that the stain be left on the surface for five to fifteen minutes and then wiped off in the direction of the grain. They recommend that a second coat of stain be applied after twelve hours. You should wait another twenty-four hours before applying a clear finish coat.

Another manufacturer, Zar, has different instructions. Here, the directions permit you to apply a second coat after only six hours and you can immediately wipe away the excess. All manufacturers provide specific details

for each of their products. Read the directions before buying a product so you will know the requirements and can choose the product that will look best for you—and will fulfill your schedule requirements.

Wiping stains, like many other products used around the home, can be hazardous; use caution. Wiping stains contain mineral spirits and petroleum distillates. They are toxic if swallowed and must be stored where small children will not find them. The stains are volatile and should be used in well-ventilated areas; avoid breathing the fumes. Never smoke while you are

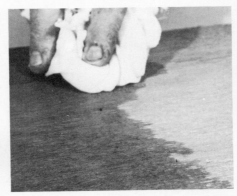

Always work stain into wood along the grain. Work wet into wet and wipe evenly to prevent unnecessary buildup of stain in one place.

using a wiping stain or use this material near an open flame. Read and follow all cautions printed on the labels.

Wiping stain has one quality that may make its use unattractive for some projects. The stain can cover and hide the grain of a wood. You will probably not want to use it on wood with attractive grain.

When you use wiping oil stain, the container will give instructions on drying times. To be prudent, however, wait at least twenty-four hours before applying a final finish to the wood. If for any reason you are concerned about whether the stain will dry to the shade you want, you can test the result by speeding up the drying in a small and inconspicuous place by drying with a hair dryer/blower. If it is too light, you can always apply additional stain after the whole piece is dry. If the color is too dark, you may lighten the surface color.

Use a hairdryer to speed drying if you testing a stain and to check the color without waiting through the natural drying time.

HOW TO LIGHTEN A DARK STAIN

Whenever you apply stain to wood, there is always the possibility of misjudging the color of the stain or the time needed between application and wiping off the excess. If the piece is too dark, simply rub the piece with the same solvent that is found in the stain. Use water for water stain, naphtha or turpentine for oil, alcohol for alcohol stain. This will lighten the wood considerably. Another way to get an even tone of stain is to apply the stain in varying strengths to different sections of the wood. The author, however, prefers lightening by simply wiping excess stain away. You can check variations and apply additional stain in some areas. This must be done carefully, but application of solvent to lighten some spots or areas should solve most problems. Remember that when a piece of furniture is standing in place in a room, few people will notice any slight discrepancies in color. If the differences are on different planes, they will be almost indiscernable. The eye does not "remember" as it moves from place to place on an object.

APPLYING A SHELLAC FINISH

Three to four coats of shellac are commonly applied as a standard finish. Shellac should be rubbed down with fine grade (000) steel wool between coats for better adherence and smoothness. When you apply shellac, remember that it is a fast drying material, and it should be worked with quickly. The rule is to use as wide a brush as possible. A 2½ inch to 3 inch natural bristle brush works well. Use a brush with fine hairs. The first coat is not particularly important but the succeeding coats are.

Step 1: Shellacking the Top Surface

Pour shellac into a wide mouth container so the brush bristles will not catch on the edge. Dip the brush about halfway into the shellac; be careful and do not create bubbles in the shellac. If you apply shellac with bubbles, they will be trapped in the surface since the shellac dries quickly. There should be a good coating on the brush so the shellac will flow off the brush. Apply the shellac in long, even strokes from one end of the piece to the other. Overlap the previously applied section for complete, even coverage. Your brush should move parallel to the previously applied section; sweep the strokes from one end of the piece to the other. Redip the brush and apply more shellac starting at one end and moving the brush smoothly to the other. Overlap the strokes slightly, so that you cover the surface in 3-inch wide sections. Strive to apply the material evenly. To work on the edges of the piece, dip the tip of the brush in the shellac and apply it in one continuous motion.

Step 2: Brushing the Turnings

Parts of some pieces will, of course, have to be handled differently from a wide, flat surface. To shellac anything that is cylindrical, such as a turning or other unusual part of furniture, use just enough shellac to coat the surface but not so much that the shellac will drip or run. Apply the shellac by moving the brush around the turning. Apply a brush-wide band, then shellac a band below it, repeating until the whole turning is covered.

If you have a small item to shellac, use small spray cans of shellac.

Draw the brush, well-loaded with shellac, along the grain of the wood. Overlap strokes to cover the surface completely and avoid "missed spots" that will show when the shellac is dry.

Apply shellac around the turnings of chair and table legs. Do not overload the brush when doing this or the shellac will run.

USING VARNISH ON FURNITURE

TECHNIQUES FOR STANDARD VARNISH

You may apply varnish at temperatures down to 65° F. The material will not flow as freely below this temperature. If you apply varnish in temperatures much greater than 85°F., it will flow too freely. There are more serious potential problems caused by the lower temperatures, because impeded flow on the surface may cause the varnish to crack or blister.

Step 1: Avoiding Dust Problems

Try to work in as dust-free environment as possible; thoroughly dust your work area the day before you begin the varnishing, and use dust covers on anything in the area that might give off dust. Precautions will prevent many problems.

Step 2: Preparing the Surface

Because varnish shows all surface imperfections, any surface to be finished with varnish must be absolutely smooth. Raise and sand down the grain until the surface is as smooth and even as you can get it. Clean all dust off and wipe with a tack rag.

It is also a good idea to have something to pick up specks of dust and lint that may float down onto the wet varnish despite your best efforts. You can use an artist's sable brush, a toothpick or, best of all, a homemade item called a pick stick.

Step 3: Making A Pick Stick

A pick stick is made from a cotton swab dipped in some specially prepared varnish. Heat some varnish in a double boiler created out of a small tin can set in a larger tin can of water. Purchase some crushed rosin from a music store and add seven or eight parts rosin to one part heated varnish. The rosin should dissolve completely.

When the varnish and rosin have been mixed, let the mixture cool and dip a cotton swab into the material and pick up a tiny amount about ⅛ inch in diameter. Moisten your fingers and roll the substance into a pear shape. Continue to roll and tap it in the palm of your hand until it is sticky but firm. The tool is now ready to use.

A useful tool to prevent problems in varnishing is a pickstick. A cotton swab is dipped into a mixture of varnish and rosin.

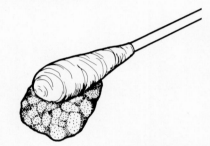

A small amount of the mixture adheres to the cotton swab and will become the pickup tool when it has been worked.

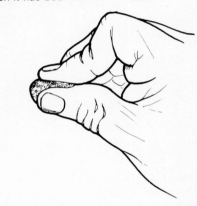

Roll the varnish/rosin mixture, along with some of the cotton, between moistened fingers until it is formed with a single point.

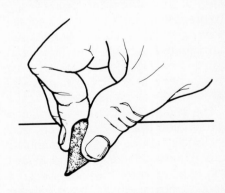

If lint or dust settles on the moist varnish, touch the pickstick to the lint, avoiding the varnished surface, and lift away the lint.

To pick the lint or dust from the wet varnish, touch the sticky mixture to the lint or dust on the surface.

Step 4: Applying the Varnish

Apply the varnish with a good-quality natural bristle brush. Dip the brush about one-third of the way into the varnish. Flow it on across the grain. To flow varnish on the surface, do not touch the wood with the brush. Use the brush to guide the varnish across the wood.

Do not stir varnish. When you dip the brush, withdraw it and just tap the bristles on the inside of the can. Never wipe the brush on the edge of the can.

When you have applied the varnish across the grain, add more by flowing it on with the grain. While the varnish is still very wet, tip it off by pulling the brush, held almost vertically, the length of the piece. Overlap your strokes. Keep a sharp eye for dust specks and pick them up right away.

You may make a mistake when you apply a first coat of varnish, because varnish becomes sticky, but not dry, quickly. In such cases, it is best to let any missed spot or other mistake dry and to correct the error when you apply the next coat.

Apply varnish across the grain in the first strokes. Allow the varnish to flow off the brush and cover the surface.

Project continued on next page

To finish to a high polish, make a paste of powdered pumice and clean motor or machine oil. Dip a smooth, clean cloth into the paste and rub it onto the wood stroking the cloth with the grain. Use another clean cloth to wipe the paste off to check your progress. The varnish should become very smooth and have a high gloss. If you want an even higher gloss, repeat the process, except use a paste made with rottenstone and oil. Always rub the paste in the direction of the grain.

USING A URETHANE VARNISH

Applying a urethane is simple. Use either a nylon or other bristle brush to flow the material on. Some manufacturers recommend that the first coat be thinned slightly with mineral spirits and that you apply as many as three coats of the urethane. This will vary from manufacturer to manufacturer

When you have covered the surface with varnish applied across the grain, immediately apply more varnish with the grain. Overlap all strokes.

Although varnish is a clear finish, some may be nearly opaque when applied. This varnish lets you see any missed area quickly.

WORKING WITH RUBBING VARNISH

If you have bought rubbing varnish, and want to achieve a very high gloss finish, you must use powdered pumice stone and perhaps rottenstone, both of which are available at paint stores. Pumice stone is just that, a volcanic stone that has been ground into a powder. Check the powder before use and remove any larger particles that could cut into the finish.

Rottenstone is limestone more finely ground than pumice. Rottenstone is used with a rubbing pad, which is a block of felt, from ¼ inch to about 1 inch thick. A blackboard eraser makes an excellent rubbing pad.

Before applying each succeeding coat of rubbing varnish, rub the var-

nished surface of the piece lightly with 0000 steel wool or extra fine sandpaper to provide a slightly rough surface, or "tooth", for the next coat.

Step 5: Smoothing the Coats

To prepare for application of a second coat, and for each additional coat, smooth the varnish with fine sandpaper or 0000 steel wool. Use the sandpaper with a light touch, and wipe the surface completely clean.

The choice of how many coats of varnish you apply is up to you, your particular tastes, and the manufacturer. If the wood has been well sealed, one coat of varnish should be sufficient on most surfaces. Two coats are preferred for greater protection, but in most cases, one coat will be enough.

and from product to product. It also will depend on whether or not you are applying the finish over new or old wood. New wood will generally require more coats, because the wood will absorb it more. On old surfaces, you will have to sand just to remove gloss before applying the new finish. Follow manufacturer's directions regarding sanding between coats and drying time between coats.

APPLYING OIL FINISHES

LINSEED OIL

To use boiled linseed oil, first dilute it with turpentine. A ratio of one third turpentine to two thirds oil is good.

Pour a small amount of oil on the wood and rub with clean, lintless cloths. Rub until all the oil has disappeared, and then use a dry cloth to wipe the surface dry. Run your hand on the surface to check that all the oil is gone. It is important to examine carved or grooved sections of the wood for hidden oil deposits; if left alone, the oil will become gummy and will collect dirt.

Boiled linseed oil had been used as an oil finish by generations of finishers. Oiled finishes are easily repaired and durable.

An application to a 4x4 foot table top should take about twenty to twenty-five minutes. After the application of the oil, use another cloth to polish the wood until the surface has a soft glow and is dry to the touch. When it is dry, allow a week for further drying, then repeat the procedure given above. A minimum of four treatments is recommended, but the number is up to you. Some finishers apply as many as ten and twelve coats and more. When you have finished each application, wash the cloths well or dispose of them carefully; linseed oil is flammable.

PENETRATING OIL

When you use penetrating oil finish, apply many coats. Rub each in well, like linseed oil. You should check each manufacturer's individual directions, but the basic procedure is to apply the oil in a circular motion with a lintless cloth, then rub the surface parallel to the grain. As each coat is finished, it is buffed with a cloth. Normally, there is a substantial waiting period between coats. Minwax, for example, advises at least 24 hours between each coat. You can use as many coats of penetrating oil as you wish; it is a matter of personal taste. However, the drying time between coats must be observed.

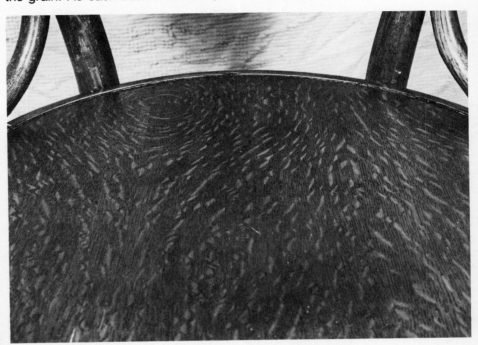

Oiled finishes often bring out grain patterns with a richness not seen in other finishes. Some woods are particularly enhanced by the application of an oil finish.

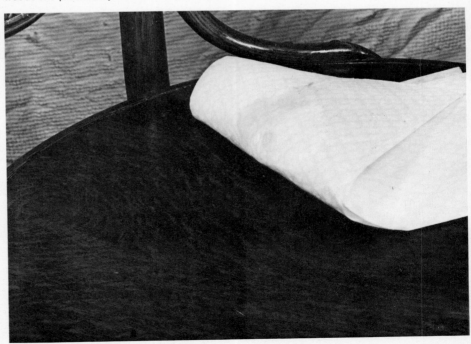

Do not rush the application of an oil finish. Apply the oil generously enough to cover the surface and then wipe away and rub the surface until no residue transfers to your cloth.

PAINTING YOUR FURNITURE

CHOOSING AND USING BRUSHES

A 2 inch or 2½ inch brush is usually the best size for painting furniture. A 2-inch brush covers an area wide enough to keep the job moving smoothly and still gives good control when working on small items such as knobs and tabletop edges. Always use a nylon brush for latex paint. For oil-base, you can use a natural bristle brush or nylon. Natural bristle may not be used with latex because water is absorbed by the bristles. The bristles swell and the paint becomes too thick to apply smoothly.

Never paint with a cheap brush. Expect to pay at least $5 or $6 for a brush. A good brush will last, be easier to clean and will not drop bristles on your freshly painted wood.

Cleaning Your Brushes

When you are finished with a brush for a day, and you will have to continue painting tomorrow, you can avoid cleaning the brush if you wrap the bristles with plastic wrap and tape the wrap so it will be airtight. The paint will stay moist and the brushes will be soft the next day.

To clean brushes used with oil-base paint in mineral spirits, pour some mineral spirits in a can and immerse the bristles in the solvent. Knead the bristles (wear gloves) to remove most of the paint. Wipe the brush against the inside of the can. Pour fresh solvent into a second can and dip the brush into the solvent to rinse. To remove the solvent, make a paste with soap and water or detergent and water and work this into the bristles. Rinse well and hang the brush to air dry; always hang with bristles down.

To clean a brush used with latex paint, wash it in warm water and soap. Wash until it is as clean as you can get it, then rinse. Do not expect to get the brush clean by just running the bristles under the water tap unless you can spend a great deal of time at it. The soap, on the other hand, lifts the paint out of the bristles quickly. Shake excess moisture from the brush and hang it to dry. If your brushes are really clean, the bristles should be smooth, flexible and undistorted when dry. If the bristles are stiff, you need to clean the brush again.

PREPARING FOR PAINTING

Before doing any preparation, remove as much hardware as you can. You may want to paint the hardware; if so paint the pieces individually. Use the same number of coats on the hardware as you use on the piece itself. Take care when painting hardware that you paint evenly. Do not use too much paint or you may create sags.

Make any needed repairs to the furniture and fill holes and gaps with wood filler. Use medium grade sandpaper to rub down the piece completely. This provides a "tooth," a slightly rougher surface, so the paint will stick. Before painting, wipe away all sanding dust with a brush moistened in the solvent that also is used as a component in the paint (check with your dealer), or with a tack rag.

PAINTING A CHAIR

To paint a chair, turn the chair upside

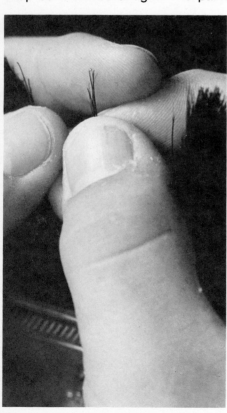

A good brush will have fine, feathered, slightly uneven bristles to hold paint. A nylon bristle is more uniform than a natural one.

If you cannot clean a brush thoroughly at the end of a painting day, you may wrap the bristles well in plastic wrap or aluminum foil. Store in a cool basement or in a refrigerator.

down and rest the seat on a box, tabletop or workbench. Paint the underside of the seat, and the legs and braces. Paint turned pieces by applying the paint in bands around the turned pieces. When you have covered the base section in this fashion, brush the paint lightly down the length of the section. Let dry. When the paint is dry, turn the chair upright and coat all top surfaces, painting the seat last.

PAINTING A TABLE

Invert the table on a raised surface. Paint the underside, if desired, and then the apron and the legs. If the legs are square, paint one side at a time. When painting smooth or turned legs, apply the paint around the width, then lightly brush lengthwise. Do not overload the brush with paint. Allow the piece to dry.

Return the table to an upright position and coat the top edges. Finish the top by applying paint in full, even strokes across the grain and then lightly brushing in the direction of the grain. Use the tip of the brush to create a smooth, even finish. Apply more coats, if needed, following the same sequence.

PAINTING CHESTS OF DRAWERS OR CABINETS

If the chest is small, turn it upside down and paint the legs first. When the legs have dried, return the chest to an upright position.

If you plan to paint the interior of the chest or cabinet, do that next, then do the drawers. If you are going to paint the inside of the drawers, do so before painting the outside face. Then coat the drawer sides to about six inches back from the front panel. Remove the knobs or pulls before painting the front panel. Even if you plan to paint the pulls, do them separately. You will have a much better-looking piece. Paint tends to run down over the hardware and create an uneven, streaked finish when the hardware is painted in place. Finish the chest by painting its sides, skirting and, finally, the top.

If the piece of furniture is too large to move or turn upside down, then you will have to paint it in place. Put news-paper around the piece and lay drop cloths over the paper. No matter how careful you are, plastic or canvas drop cloths should be used to protect all surrounding areas. Wipe your feet each time you leave the work area or lay down a newspaper path where you expect to walk. It is easy to pick up a spot or two of paint on the sole of a shoe and to track the paint onto a finished floor or a section of carpeting.

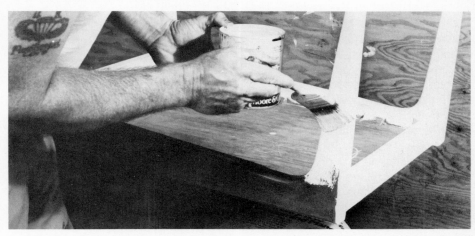

Paint legs and underside (if desired) first. Invert furniture to do this whenever possible. This will make the process easier for you and less likely to spatter your floor.

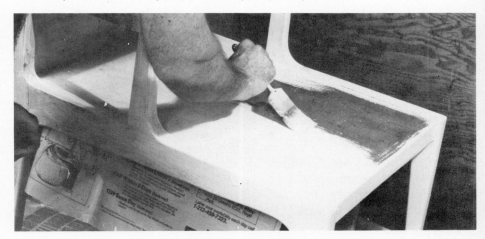

Top surfaces should be done last. Use a well loaded brush for smooth application, but do not apply too much in one stroke or your paint may run, sag or puddle.

Because the grain should not show, the direction of your strokes is not important. Apply coats in alternate directions but finish by brushing final coat in both directions while wet.

USING A SPRAY PAINT

You can apply spray paint from small cans or with a rented spray applicator. Spraying will almost certainly enable you to achieve a finish that is smoother than you could attain with a brush, because it delivers a perfectly even amount of paint to the surface. That is, if you use the gun properly, the same amount of paint (or other material) will be applied to the surface at all times. Unless you are a master painter, you will undoubtedly apply more paint in one area than another. This may not be important if the variation is slight. It is possible to apply a very smooth finish with a brush. The only situation where a spray is the only sure way to produce a smooth finish, in the opinion of the author, is when using lacquer. This material dries so rapidly that brush application usually will mean you will have visible brush marks; spray is a much better choice.

PAINT FROM A SPRAY CAN
If you use a spray can, it is important to remember that a number of light coats gives better coverage than application of just one or two heavy coats. When you spray on a heavy coat there is always a tendency for the paint to sag and run.

Step 1: Positioning the Furniture
If possible, set the item so that it can be sprayed horizontally; this will to some degree help keep the paint from running.

Step 2: Spraying the Unit
Shake the can according to directions. Then depress the nozzle to allow the first spray to escape onto a piece of newspaper. Position the nozzle about 8 inches from the item to be sprayed and a little to the left or right of it (depending on whether you are right or left handed). Press the button to start the spray and then move the can so that the spray hits the item you are painting. In other words, the spray should be on fully and moving before the expelled paint contacts the item. Keep moving the can across the wood, not lingering in one spot. Lingering can cause a buildup that can cause sags. When you want to stop, move the can

so the spray is past the item you are painting before you stop the spray.

Make another pass, which overlaps the first by a few inches. Progressively spray with additional passes, overlapping each of the previous ones until the material has built up to a solid color. Let each coat dry before you apply the next.

Step 3: Coating Remaining Surfaces
If you are spraying a piece that involves doing more than one side, let each plane dry completely before doing additional coats.

HANDLING A SPRAY UNIT
You can buy or rent a spray unit. However, this should only be a consideration if you have a lot of work or a large job in order to justify the cost.

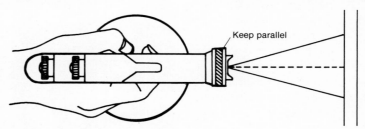

Keep parallel

There are two types of paint sprayers available. One of the most common styles houses paint in a closed container. Compressed air is forced through a hose to a spray gun. The paint is atomized as it is forced out the cap of the spray gun.

The second type of spray gun is "airless." In this unit, a hydraulic pump rather than air pressure forces the paint out through a fine strainer at very high pressure. The spray comes out thicker and it is easier to do a good job with this type.

There are several points to keep in mind when setting up and using spray equipment. In an air sprayer, the paint must be thin enough to be atomized and turned into a spray, but thick enough to stick to a surface without running or dripping. The air pressure on the jar of paint determines exactly how much paint will flow into the nozzle. The air cap on the spray gun controls the amount and distribution of air and how it mixes with the paint; there

are different caps for different materials. The nozzle on the spray gun controls the amount of paint and air delivered to the surface. If too much air is fed in, the paint will atomize too much and a fine, dry spray will be produced. If too little pressure is applied, the paint spatters and leaves a speckled, almost gritty, coat. The paint's thickness should be changed only if necessary.

Specific directions will be available with each unit. If you are renting a unit, discuss with the rental agent what you will be using and he will help you determine pressure settings.

Hold the spray gun 6 to 10 inches away from the surface to be painted. If it is held much farther away, the spray will "dust"; that is, the droplets will dry up in midair and hit the surface as hard, solid particles. Keep the spray gun at right angles to the surface to be covered. It should be straight up and down and not tilted. Move your arm back and forth parallel to the surface. The spray pattern should feather, overlapping without definable (sharp) edges. To assure an even transition, pull the trigger on the gun after the stroke begins and release it before it ends. At corners, stop the paint 1 to 2 inches before the corner. Then sweep the gun up and down the corner so that both sides are hit at the same time.

Air-gun spray painting either should be done outside or in an area where you will not be concerned about airborne paint mist settling on surfaces. The airless sprayer does not present this problem. With the air-gun sprayer there is really no way to cover up adequately against mist. One possible alternative is to build a spray booth from cardboard. Always wear a breathing mask or respirator when spray painting indoors.

6
Specialty Finishes

The glass-like finish of a French polish shows the wood to advantage and creates a reflective display surface for favorite objects.

Although most furniture pieces are finished with a simple shellac, lacquer or varnish coating, several special finishes may be more appropriate for certain types and styles of furniture. For example, the piece may be of wood that is so uniquely attractive that a simple varnish may not seem good enough. Other pieces, even after careful removal of an old finish, sanding and preparation, may not be sufficiently attractive to stand up to examination through a clear finish. However, these pieces may still seem too interesting to be finished with plain paint. The alternatives presented here include: French polish, "distressing", and special painting techniques (step-by-step techniques follow later).

FRENCH POLISH
This finish is difficult, tiring and time-consuming to apply. However, it is worth the effort if the piece to which it is applied will be markedly improved.

The finish created with a French polish is high-gloss and lustrous. When properly done, a French polish will create the impression that the surface was dipped in glass.

A true French polish takes many weeks and many steps to achieve. The do-it-yourselfer can achieve an attractive, high-gloss finish that will look like a true French polish—but lack its depth and durability—with less effort and time. However, the word "less" is used

Distressing wood may increase the visual interest of the grain. If you fill scratches, holes and dents with contrasting filler, apply a smooth, clear finish to retain distressed appearance.

Turned spindles may accept highlighting for dramatic effect. This technique is especially effective on light finishes and on certain pieces of 18th century-style furniture.

here as a relative term. A French polish, even approximated, takes time and effort. Most refinishers would say that it takes "elbow grease".

DISTRESSING

Occasionally, a piece will strip down to a clean surface that reveals more aging and wear than you anticipated. You may find the scratches deeper and more frequent than you expected. You may find that the edges are worn, chipped or cracked. You may, of course, repair all of these problems as detailed in Chapter 3. However, you may also find that you can make the most of these problems by incorporating them into the finish to create a "distressed finish." You may: add more marks, scratches and mars to the surface; wear down the edges farther; burn or char the surface carefully for effect. You can even rub stains into the wood.

SPECIAL PAINTING TECHNIQUES

There are some woods whose characters are such that, in their basic appearances, they offer no visual interest and adds nothing to the impression of the form and lines of the piece of furniture. In these cases, you may want to use a paint finish that features additional detailing or finishing techniques.

Highlighting

This technique usually incorporates a gold or silver metallic finish applied to certain areas of a piece of furniture. These areas are usually the edges, legs or turnings, and decorative detailing or molding. In some cases, the highlighting may be very subtle. The metallic finish, usually a powder suspended in an oil/turpentine mixture or in a varnish, is applied with a brush and then wiped off after a few minutes. The metallic material remains in the carving and deep areas of the turnings. If you apply the metallic finish with a rag wrung nearly dry, the metal gleam will reflect off the raised areas of the wood.

Mottling

This technique may use two paints, a paint and a stain, an opaque and clear stain, or a paint and a glaze. The base coat is applied and allowed to dry. The second color material is applied with a nearly dry sponge, rolled or wadded cloth, or even a piece of heavy, absorbent paper or plastic. The result is a varied visual texture that adds depth and interest to the surface.

Pickling

A popular finish technique in the 19th century, pickling bleached the wood with caustic solutions. The same effect can be created with safer, contemporary materials using a sealer and a wiping coat of white enamel. In many respects, pickling is the reverse of antiquing.

Antiquing

The popularity of antiquing has waned recently, but it is an attractive finish. Appropriate for certain period furniture pieces, the light background is coated with a darker, transparent finish that is wiped off. The residue remains in light or dark streaks and in corners and carvings.

Graining

This technique simulates wood grain, usually on painted wood. In skillful, professional hands, the grain of one wood can be simulated on another wood. There are kits that allow graining to be done rapidly by using a "comb" pulled through a semi-transparent glazing coat. However, there are other ways to simulate grain through the use of various brushes and colors. The technique is described in the project section.

Surface Texturing

Although creating a texture on the surface of a piece of furniture is a rare choice, you may create a simulated travertine or rough slate surface on a table if you wish by applying a plaster coat and working the surface to simulate the desired finish.

Decoupage

This technique of applying colorful printed pictures is usually used for trays and plaques, but is also popular for decorating certain styles of chairs and dressers. The printed piece is coated many times with varnish or other sealer until a smooth finished surface is achieved.

Stenciling

Although many people think of stenciling in terms of a simple, flat design, stencils may be combined to achieve various patterns. Stenciling was a popular finishing craft during the colonial period; a stenciled border or center decoration may be particularly appropriate and attractive on these pieces of furniture.

Hand Painting

Both European and Oriental traditions use decorative hand painting. Some techniques, such as rosemaling, a Norwegian decorative tradition, are used on furniture. Various Chinese- and Japanese-inspired furniture are candidates for hand-done decorative painting. The limitation on this is your own artistic skill.

This old chest was given an antique finish to emphasize the unusual carved moldings. The original finish was badly alligatored.

A stencil, in a design appropriate to the room decor, may add considerably to the appearance of a piece of furniture.

The decoration on this box is decoupage. Various types of printed material may be used for this decoration. The paper is glued to the box and then coated over and over with varnish.

APPLYING A FRENCH POLISH

A French polish is a shellac applied in many, many layers with a soft, padded cotton "rubber." After each application of shellac has dried, the surface is smoothed with oil and an abrasive before a new layer of shellac is added.

PREPARING THE SURFACE
Because this finish is meant to create a mirror-smooth surface, the wood must be carefully prepared to receive the shellac.

Step 1: Sanding and Raising the Grain
Sand the wood, raise the grain and resand until the wood does not expand and the grain does not rise when moisture is applied to the surface.

Step 2: Sealing the Wood
To prevent any possible raising of the grain after you begin the French polishing process, apply a sealer to the wood. Apply the sealer coat, which is a thin application of shellac, with a wad of cotton gauze wrapped in a lint-free cotton cloth. This padding is very much like the rubber you will use for the polish process. The cloth wrapped around the gauze wad should be free of wrinkles and very smooth.

Step 3: Filling the Wood
To fill all the pores, use a wood filler tinted to blend with or to match the wood. Some finishes use a plaster filler tinted with powdered colors. The English method of French polishing traditionally uses a plaster filler.

Apply the filler with a cloth, rubbing the surface with considerable pressure to force the filler into the pores. Let the filler dry completely.

Step 4: Sanding the Surface
Sand with a very fine wet-dry sandpaper moistened with boiled linseed oil. If possible, use an old, soft piece of sandpaper. Use only enough oil to moisten the paper and to keep it soft.

Step 5: Staining the Wood
A piece of furniture given a French polish should have an even color finish. That is, there should not be any

The first stage in a French polish is sanding the wood. This may take time. You must remove or fill deep scratches or dents and provide an even surface for the many layers of shellac.

After sanding the wood should be given a coat of sealer. This will prevent the grain rising and giving you an uneven surface on which to work. You can now begin to apply the shellac.

noticeable variation in the intensity of the color on the wood. The eye should move across the surface without the visual interruption of changes in color or tone.

Apply the stain with great care. Before applying the stain to a piece of furniture you are working on, practice on a piece of scrap wood until you are sure of how much stain to apply, how long to leave it on, and how much to wipe off.

When you have applied the stain, the surface should be very smooth and the color of the wood very rich. You will now enhance this look with the French polish.

CREATING THE FRENCH POLISH
Step 1: Making the Rubber
The only tool you will use in applying the French polish is the rubber. This is a wadded gauze or cheesecloth covered with a piece of lint-free cotton cloth. The center portion of the rubber, the wadded cheesecloth, is called a "fad". To make the fad, fold the gauze or cheesecloth, tucking the corners and edges around to one side. Mold the fad into a pear-shaped wad that will fit comfortably into your hand. This is the part of the rubber that will be moistened with the shellac.

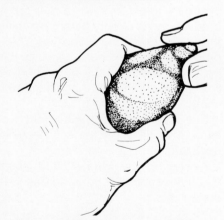

The foundation of the French polish is the cotton wad inside the cloth cover, the "fad". It holds the "charge" of shellac.

Cover the fad with a piece of lintless cotton cloth. Wrap this soft cloth carefully around the fad. Tuck the ends of this outer cloth around the fad and pull the face side smooth. Any wrinkles that may occur in this outer cloth will leave marks on the surface of the shel-

The fad is covered by lintless cotton cloth. This cloth must be soft but firm so that it may be wrapped around the fad and not have any tendency to draw into wrinkles. The rubber must be smooth or your polish will ripple.

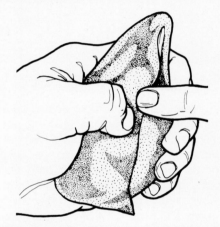

Wrap the cloth around the fad and tuck all excess into a seam. You will have to refold the cloth each time you add shellac.

When you have finished wrapping the cloth, you should have a rubber that conforms to the shape of the fad and is completely smooth.

lac finish. You will have to check the rubber frequently to be sure that its surface is always smooth.

Step 2: Mixing the Shellac
Various wood finishers have created different formulae, which they have settled on after experience in applying a French polish. However, our experience has led to the conclusion that a very thin mixture is best for the novice finisher. A thin solution made up of one pound of shellac flakes in one gallon of alcohol (a one pound cut) will go onto the surface very smoothly and be less likely to show ridges or marks. If you have never attempted a French polish before, this thin mixture will be more forgiving of any mistakes. However, you will take more time in applying the extra coats of shellac to build up the finish. This is balanced by the fact that you will spend far less time than if you had to correct many "errors", such as uneven application of shellac or ridges created by overlapping thick wet shellac on a section where the shellac had already dried.

The "classic" formula is only a little thicker—a mixture of 1½ pounds of shellac flakes in one gallon of alcohol. Some finishers, professionals with a lot of experience with French polish application, use cuts of 2½ pounds to as thick as 4 pounds.

Step 3: Applying the Polish
Dip the fad of the rubber in the shellac and squeeze out the excess. The material should be wet but not dripping. Then wrap the fad in the outer cloth, making the surface as smooth as possible. Unwrap the fad each time you put more shellac on the inner wadding.

Proper Polishing Motion There are three arm motions used to apply the shellac polish. The first is circular; the second is a figure 8; the third is a straight motion following the grain of the wood. The shellac is applied and polished primarily with the circular and figure 8 patterns. The straight strokes are followed by the circular and/or figure 8 strokes. Do not use too many straight strokes or fail to follow the straight strokes with the circular strokes. If you do, the shellac (even

Project continued on next page

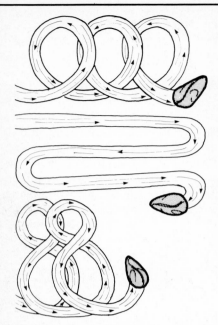

Apply the polish with a series of motions each time you charge the fad. Begin the motion while your hand is above the surface so you contact the surface while your hand is moving. Use all the motions shown above.

When you have finished the final step of the French polish, you should have a completely smooth surface with a mirror-like finish that will enhance the appearance of the wood.

thin shellac) will build up noticeable lines or ridges of shellac on the surface. These will have to be sanded out or the surface will be ruined.

Contacting the Surface Begin making circular strokes in the air above the surface. Slowly lower your arm while continuing the circular motion. Keep your arm moving at all times. Do not apply pressure on the surface when you make contact; pressure will force the shellac out of the rubber unevenly. You must try to apply the shellac evenly, with each stroke identical in pressure to the one before.

Lifting the Rubber from the Surface When you feel the rubber start to pull lightly on the surface, you should "recharge" the fad with more shellac. If you lift the rubber straight up, it will leave a rough spot on the surface. Continue to make the circular motion and move the rubber lightly over the surface, so that you can lift your arm as the rubber reaches the edge.

Step 4: Covering the Surface

Keep working until you have applied the shellac polish to one entire surface of the piece you are working on. If you are doing a table or a desk, complete the entire top before you stop. A din-

ing room table may have a division in the center to accept leaves so that you can do one section at a time, but you must complete the shellac application for an entire section each time you work. If you stop and try to finish the section later, there will be a ridge where the two applications of shellac overlap.

Step 5: Sanding between Coats

After a section has been coated with the shellac, allow the finish to dry. The minimum safe drying time is three hours. If possible, allow the shellac to dry overnight. Since the entire process of creating a French polish will take a long time, it is foolish to attempt to rush any one part of the process.

When the shellac is dry, sand the surface with a fine sandpaper. You may put a drop of oil on the sandpaper; however, this is not necessary when sanding between the first two or three coats.

Wipe the surface clean with a soft cloth and then with a tack rag. Any dust left on the surface will show up and mar the French polish.

Step 6: Completing the French Polish

Repeat the application of shellac and sanding in the same careful manner until you have applied several coats. You may apply as few as four coats or as many as twenty before reaching the point where the wood has taken on a deep and lustrous sheen. At this point you should add a drop of boiled linseed oil to the fad each time you charge it with shellac.

Use fine sandpaper with a drop of oil on it to sand the surface between applications of shellac.

Achieving the Final Polish When you have applied, let dry, and sanded enough coats so that the wood is rich looking and the surface smooth and slick, apply a fine lubricating oil to the surface and sprinkle a small amount of rottenstone over the oil. Use a soft cloth or a soft block—such as a clean felt blackboard eraser or a block of cork, wrapped in a soft, lint-free cloth—to polish the surface to the final, glass-like finish.

Natural wood floors and paneling are an asset to a home. Proper care and maintenance will protect and preserve the material indefinitely.

After years of wear, a wood floor can be renewed. Just strip and refinish. The natural wood will respond to the treatment with a fresh look.

A finish should be applied to protect a wood floor. The wood may be stained to enhance the wood grain and then protected with varnish.

Wood fits in any setting. This old oak washstand is in a contemporary home. Varnish or an oil finish protects wood from moisture.

Different woods can be made compatible through the use of stain. Here the woodwork has been stained to blend with the lavatory vanity.

When this cabinet was stripped of paint, some was left in grooves and crevices rather than risking damage from digging with pointed tools.

There are many varieties of stain available to the finisher/refinisher. Some, like that being used here, also seal the wood.

Any furniture is a candidate for refinishing. This piano, now scarred and cracked, responds immediately to the remover.

Bare wood is enlivened with stain. A plain rocking chair becomes more attractive as the stain is applied to the wood.

Paint and natural wood finishes combine well. Here the eye is lead up the stairs and to the leaded window by the lines of the railing.

Differing architectural elements are made more unified with light paint. The dark finish on the floor and railing receives the attention.

The classic moldings in this room have been painted to contrast with the walls and to focus attention on the architectural details.

The modern, glass-top table and the Queen Anne chairs are painted the same dramatic color so the difference in style is less apparent.

Painted woodwork unifies the decorating scheme in this room and allows the natural wood of the furniture to become the primary interest.

Various handpainting techniques were used here to create the distinctive cabinet fronts that coordinate with the wallpaper in this kitchen.

This antique chair is decorated extensively. The subtle colors modify the impression made by the bold, decorative style of painting.

A more delicate decoration is used on this spice rack. Small hand-detail work is combined with a stencil-like pattern at the top.

This child's rocking reindeer is decorated with swirled mottling. This can be done with a cloth, sponge, rag or even plastic wrap.

Faux marbre, hand-painted imitation marble and a popular technique in the 19th century, gives an elegant look to simple wood. Considerable practice is required to perfect the technique.

Rough-sawn cabinet fronts and smooth finished beams and woodwork in this room are unified through the use of similar colors and antiquing.

Rough-sawn and antiqued finishes are combined in this kitchen. Varnish applied over the antiqued counter will protect it from wear.

Although highlighting is usually done with gold or silver, an attractive highlight can be obtained with the use of ordinary paint. The green used here coordinates with the room decor.

To highlight a piece of molding, you must apply a solid, smooth basecoat. The effect is more noticeable on a white or pastel basecoat.

The entire surface of the molding is coated with the metallic paint. Dry-brush application may be used, but it is more difficult.

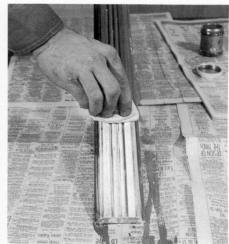

After the metallic glaze has set for a very few minutes, use a clean, soft rag to wipe away the paint on the smooth, flat surfaces.

Although this piece is from a commercial manufacturer; it is possible for a skilled do-it-yourselfer to approximate this chinoiserie style.

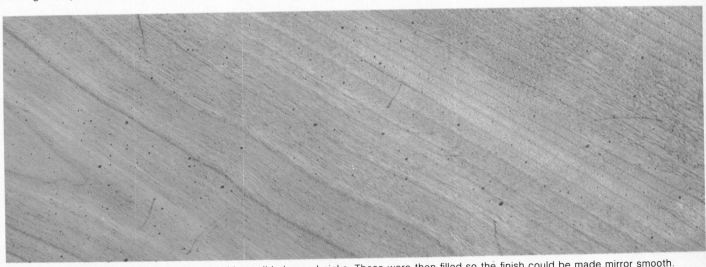

This tabletop was given a distressed finish with small holes and nicks. These were then filled so the finish could be made mirror smooth.

This old storage unit was given new life when the surface was redone in an antiqued finish applied directly over the old surface.

1 The work begins with basecoating. Here, pink is used, and, because it is lighter than the existing color, two coats may be needed.

4 Glaze is wiped off with a soft, clean rag. The amount removed is a matter of taste. The longer glaze sets, the less can be removed.

5 A "grain" pattern can be created by wiping the glaze in one direction. Use a fresh surface with each stroke. Have several rags.

2 The basecoat used for this project was a latex. The advantage of this material is the relative ease of application and cleanup.

3 When the basecoat is dry, the glaze coat is applied. This is a dark but transparent coating, usually varnish, that will be lightened.

6 Stroking the glaze with a clean paintbrush will further lighten and modify the glaze pattern. Wipe the brush clean after each stroke. Using a dry brush in this way will produce a finish that has a look of grained wood. Draw the brush in one direction each time.

A cabinet may be decorated with decoupage. Here a section of the wallpaper has been cut out and applied as decoration to the cabinet panels.

HOW TO DISTRESS WOOD FURNITURE

Sometimes a good piece of furniture has received very heavy wear over a period of time. This use may have resulted in serious wear at the edges, as well as dents in the surface and scrapes across the grain of the wood. You can, of course, raise the dents, fill the scrapes and rebuild the edges. However, this process may be lengthy and often will not create the type of finish base you really want or need. In certain cases, it is better to make use of the wear marks by increasing and enhancing these problems in order to turn them to your advantage.

HOW TO SHAVE EDGES

Few pieces of furniture wear evenly. If your piece has one worn edge, you may want to create another to increase the impression of an old, worn piece of furniture.

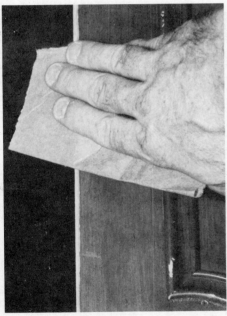

To disguise badly worn edges on a piece of furniture, you may distress the edges by sanding them down to make them more even.

Corners are subject to more wear and abuse than long edges. Curved legs and feet will become worn and kicked. The corners of drawers, especially if they are not closed tightly all the time, will wear down. The same is true of the wood around drawer pulls, especially round knobs. After many, many years of use and of fingers and knuckles pressing against the face of the drawer when the knob is pulled, the areas surrounding the knobs will get increased wear.

Tools for Shaving Edges

There are two types of tools to use in shaving edges. One type of tool wears roughly by scratching or scraping the wood; the other type trims off thin layers of wood.

Scrapers The scraping tools are primarily rasps. They are bars of metal attached to a handle. The metal bars have sharp teeth that dig into wood and wear it away. The rasp usually has one flat side and one rounded side.

Rasps come in varying degrees of roughness. When you draw a rasp across the surface of an edge of a board or tabletop, a considerable amount of material is gouged out by the rasp.

A rasp or Surform may be used to wear away edges of a piece of furniture. Check your progress regularly avoid cutting away too much.

Files are similar to rasps, but they are generally much finer. Their action is more like sandpaper. Woodworking files have handles and some are even made with a flat and a rounded side.

The Stanley Tool Company makes a device called a Surform. This is similar to a rasp except that the bar is hollow and the teeth are made so that the wood scraped away is drawn into the hollow bar. This is a much neater tool to use than the rasp.

Trimmers These tools shave away rather than wear down the wood. Trimmers of use in distressing wood are the plane, the spokeshave and the Exacto or utility knife.

A plane will cut thin layers of wood. The blade may be adjusted to cut at various thicknesses, but all thicknesses are very thin. Drawn along the sharp point where edge and top faces of a board or tabletop meet, the plane will trim off the wood quickly and smoothly. If you apply heavy or even pressure, the plane will catch in the wood and leave small nicks. If you are distressing the wood, these nicks may be desirable.

A spokeshave is a tool designed for trimming curved edges and rounded wood. This is a rather specialized tool for the average home craftsman, but you may be able to rent or borrow a spokeshave. It can save you a great deal of time if the piece of furniture you are working on has many curved or rounded edges or turned and curved legs.

A sharp knife, either a utility, matte or Exacto knife, also may be used to

You may also scrape or wear down any rounded sections of the furniture. Try to make all your work look like the results of natural wear and tear. Do not overdo the distressing.

Project continued on next page

trim and shave edges of furniture. If this is the only tool you use, your work will take some time. However, the fine, sharp knife makes the trimming easier.

Avoiding Mistakes

Look over the piece of furniture before you start and plan where you want to shave off the wood. Use a soft graphic pencil or piece of charcoal to mark the areas. Once you have marked the piece, study it for some time. Work slowly, wearing or cutting away small pieces. Practice cutting on a hidden edge so that you get the feel of the pressure needed to get the cut you want. Stop before you get too far. You cannot put back the pieces you cut away without going to a great deal of trouble. Watch the balance of the cuts. You do not want to spend a lot of time "evening up" your work.

DENTING AND CUTTING THE WOOD

Old pieces of furniture have many little dents and small gouges. There are many ways to add these marks to furniture. The classic way to dent furniture is to hit it with a length of chain. We suggest you practice on pieces of scrap wood before you try this. You want to create dents, not to leave the impression of the chain on the surface. If your piece of furniture is made of a wood that is soft, such as pine, you do not have to hit it very hard. On the other hand, if you are trying to dent oak, you will have to apply a great deal of pressure.

Another way to dent the surface of furniture is to hit it with a ballpeen hammer. You may also drill tiny holes in the surface with a very small drill bit, or use a hammer and a countersink. Small scratches may be made with a knife, and larger scratches may be made with the corner of a hammer claw. An enthusiastic child can dent almost any surface with a wooden mallet or a toy car.

As you work, check the results frequently. The furniture should look aged, not shattered.

You may add dents to the surface with a hammer or a mallet. Be careful not to strike the wood so hard that you shatter the section.

Minor scratches and small holes may be made with nails. If you have made too many, fill some with wood filler before finishing.

After charring, rub away loose material. Scrub the wood lightly with a fine wire brush until the color reaches the intensity you want.

If you are planning to apply a final clear finish, you may want to char the wood to create a variation in color. Work out-of-doors and have a fire extinguisher at hand.

BURNING THE SURFACE

This technique is of limited use. It should be tried only on clean wood. If you attempt to burn a piece of furniture that has any finish or residue of stripping on it, you will find the piece engulfed in flames because the finish or stripper residue will burn.

Work out of doors with a small torch. Hold the flame far enough away from the wood so you can control the charring. What you are trying to do is darken edges, carving and turnings. Move the flame of the torch back and forth over the areas you want to char. You do not want to burn the wood.

After you have charred an area, use a stiff brush to rub the loose material off the wood. Do not scrub the surface vigorously, but use enough strength to brush off any charred wood that could flake off. If the surface seems too dark for your purposes, you can sand the charred area lightly to remove more of the burned color. Use this technique only when you plan to finish the furniture in a clear finish.

GIVING THE FINAL FINISH

You may alter the appearance of the furniture in several ways. Distressed furniture is usually given a final clear finish; however, you may stain the wood, or even rub powdered color on the wood to achieve a certain look. A high-gloss finish can be put on distressed furniture if you fill the dents, scratches and gouges. The visual impression of the distress marks will still be retained if you fill the wood with a contrasting color.

If you are distressing a piece of furniture because it was already worn, try to use a durable finish coat such as a urethane varnish to prevent further wear and deterioration of the wood.

This cabinet is now ready for renewal. The finished surface will show the distressing, but the effect will be softened.

A wiping stain was applied to this cabinet as a first step to get the desired finish. The stain blends the marks and mars into the surface, but more will settle in the dents.

Check the stain to determine when the color has reached the intensity you want. You may achieve a grain pattern; wipe stain in one direction then brush the marks with a dry brush.

The final step is the application of a clear, protective coating. A varnish will be water resistant and still show the distressing.

SPECIALTY PAINT FINISHES

There are some pieces of furniture and certain styles of decor that are enhanced by a painted finish. On other pieces of furniture, no finish except paint is worthwhile. Properly applied, a plain painted finish can be very attractive. However, in large expanses the total sameness of the tone can look dull.

The problem of plain or dull painted furniture can be overcome or compensated for in a number of ways with the techniques offered here. Some techniques are unexpectedly easy to apply; others are more difficult. You are the best judge of whether a piece of furniture is worth the time and effort required to achieve a given effect.

HIGHLIGHTING

There are several ways to achieve highlighting. In general, the material used is a metallic paint—gold, silver or any of a number of bronze or copper variations.

If a piece of furniture has a series of decorative grooves, you may apply a line of the highlighting paint to the inside of the grooves with a small, fine brush, or use a larger brush to spread the metallic finish on turnings and carvings. Wipe the surface with a soft cloth after the metallic finish has set for a few minutes. This will leave the metallic paint in the grooves and low sections of the carving.

Another method of application calls for a soft cloth instead of a brush. Dip the cloth in the paint and squeeze the paint into the cloth. Wipe the cloth over the surface of the furniture carvings, turnings and edges. This will lay down a light metallic coating on the raised surfaces. If the effect is too light, you can wipe on a second coat. If the result is too intense, use a clean cloth to wipe off part of the paint.

MOTTLING

There are several ways to achieve a mottled look on painted wood. One way is to apply a second color with a sponge dipped in paint, stain, varnish, or shellac, adding it as a second coat. Squeeze the sponge nearly dry

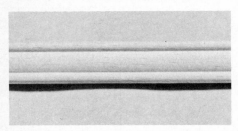

A piece of molding or a carved table edge shows how the application of highlighting can enhance the impression of the wood detailing.

After applying a smooth basecoating to the wood, a full covering of metallic or other contrasting paint is applied to the surface.

After the highlight has set but not dried, wipe it off with a soft cloth or sturdy paper towel. If you wipe off too much; try again.

A mottled finish may be created by applying a contrasting finish to a basecoat. Here a dark, transparent glaze was applied with crumpled paper to a light, thoroughly dry basecoat.

A light-color glaze applied over a darker basecoat gives the surface a "pickled" finish. This once required lye and other harsh chemicals to bleach some natural color from dark wood.

and blot the surface of the piece of furniture. If the first coat is still damp, the colors will mix and you will get a very different effect than if the second coat is applied to dry paint. If the colors are similar, the surface will have a subtle variation in visual texture. If the colors are different, the visual effect will be more dramatic.

Other materials that are effective for mottling a surface are soft paper, cloth (burlap, canvas, or rough knitted fabric), an old shaving brush (the ends of the bristles are set straight down on the wood with light pressure), crum-pled newsprint, wallpaper, wax paper, or even plastic wrap.

This is a technique that must be practiced before it is applied to a piece of furniture. Basecoat a piece of scrap lumber or a section of plywood. Test your color choice and mottling tool until you are satisfied that you have the color and markings you want. Then practice until you can fully control the mottling process.

PICKLING
To achieve a pickled finish, basecoat the wood with the color of your choice and let it dry. Apply a thin coat of white enamel. Let this coat stand a few minutes and then wipe off the white coat. A thin, white glaze will remain. This is a variation on highlighting and the opposite of antiquing.

If your basecoat is very dark, the white will be an enormous contrast; you will probably decide to wipe off most of the white.

Test the effect on scrap before using this technique on your furniture. The pickling may be very attractive on a smaller piece but, because it is so unusual, it may be disconcerting on a large piece.

ANTIQUING
Although this finishing technique is not as popular now as it was a few years ago, antiquing is effective on French provincial style furniture and also helps disguise many surface problems.

The process requires the application of a good basecoat, usually of a white or other light color. When this coat is dry, a transparent or semi-transparent glaze coat is brushed or wiped on the surface. The coat is relatively thin and is wiped off within a few minutes of application. If you wipe the glaze coat off with a brush, the surface will retain light streaks of the glaze to give the surface a lightly grained finish.

If applied with a brush, the glaze will concentrate in all grooves, turnings and ridges to produce considerable depth to the details. If you wish to apply the glaze with a soft cloth, you will find that the grooves and turnings remain free of the glaze and the raised portions of the surface are, in effect, shadowed by the glaze.

The glaze material comes in both light and dark colors from some manufacturers. You may use a stain over the paint if your main concern is to soften and to age the appearance of the paint. Test this on a piece of scrap lumber before applying it to the furniture.

Some manufacturers advise sealing the glaze coat with a clear sealer. This preserves the surface and protects it from wear. One manufacturer, however, produces an antiquing finish that is applied in one step.

An antique finish uses a darker glaze coat over a light base. The glaze may be transparent or opaque and should be applied evenly to the surface.

After the glaze coat has set for a short time, but has not dried, use a cloth, paper towel or dry brush to wipe away some or nearly all of the glaze to reveal part of the basecoat.

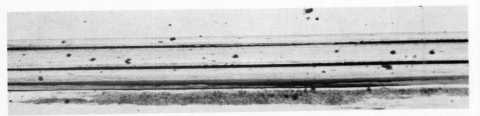

Distressed wood pinholes can be created by spattering the surface with glaze after the first application has been wiped off. Hold the brush over the surface and slap it smartly.

IMITATION WOOD GRAIN

This finishing technique was extremely popular in Victorian homes. Craftsmen of the period were able to simulate the tone and grain of very expensive fine woods on the surfaces of very inexpensive, common woods. The graining was used largely on woodwork in homes to make the interior look more elegant and more expensive than it was.

There are two methods of producing a grained finish: Kits and brushes. The first is relatively simple, although it will take some practice to get the desired results. The second method approaches the techniques of the fine, 19th century craftsmen and take time to develop as a skill. However, the results can be superior.

GRAINING WITH A KIT

The graining kits are similar to the basic antiquing kits except that the color combinations are wood tones. For example, to simulate the grain of oak, you purchase a kit designated for the shade of oak finish you desire. The basic work sequence is:

(1) practice on a hidden section or a piece of scrap;

(2) apply the basecoat with a regular paint brush;

(3) when the first coat is dry, apply the glaze coat;

(4) as soon as the glaze coat has been applied, draw a graining comb down the surface, scratching the glaze to leave "grain" marks;

(5) smooth the ridges (although the glaze is thin, the comb creates discernible ridges) by stroking the surface lightly with a fine putty knife—or use the classic tool of the grain-maker, a turkey feather;

(6) If you are dissatisfied with the effect, wipe off the glaze before it sets and try again.

GRAINING WITH A BRUSH

It is also possible to achieve a look of wood grain using paint and a brush.

Step 1: Laying the BaseCoat

Begin brushing on a flat basecoat in a color that is close to the basic wood tone you are trying to simulate. Let this coat dry before applying the grain.

Old, battered and unevenly finished, this small stool has a natural grain pattern too large for the small size of the piece.

The first step is covering the surface with a coat of paint. In this case, neutral beige.

Step 2: Choosing Colors for the Grain

For the grain, you may use acrylic paint sold in art supply stores. These water-base acrylic paint colors dry to a durable and permanent finish. This type of paint comes in a wide range of colors that can be mixed.

You will not, unless you have the talent of Rembrandt, be able to match the grain of a wood exactly. However, a close examination of a wood you want to simulate will give you an idea of the color tones in the wood. Decide on at least two shades that will approximate the look of the actual grain. Since you will have to practice before working on your furniture, you can

check the appearance as you test the colors, and if necessary you can change your mind about the color tones.

Step 3: Mixing the Graining Paint

Acrylic paints may be mixed with water, a gel, and an opaque medium. For the graining, you should use gel, available where the paint is purchased, and water. The paint should be semi-transparent for the best effect on the wood. It should be thinned so that it is smooth but not runny; it should coat the brush with a thin film.

Step 4: Practicing the Grain Pattern

Before you apply graining with a brush, carefully study the pattern of the wood grain you are trying to simulate. Practice on scrap wood until you can duplicate the swirls and wavy lines of the desired wood.

Step 5: Adding the Grain

Using the darker of the two tones you have chosen, dip a brush that is 2 or 3 inches wide into the paint and then wipe the brush nearly dry. Move the brush in one direction only; always start from the same side of the section of furniture on which you are working.

A virtually dry brush is used to apply the first grain strokes. The material was a light-color oil stain brushed in one direction.

The brush should touch the surface only lightly.

Grain is seldom perfectly straight. Do not worry if your hand wavers as you pull the brush across the surface. Put down very little paint with each stroke. If the grain appears too light, you can apply another stroke over the first. Keep the brush strokes light and the brush very dry.

After the first coating of grain has dried—in about one hour—you can apply a second coat in another color. This second coat should be in a lighter tone, but it should not be drastically different from the first graining color or much lighter than the base coat. Again, apply this coat with a nearly dry brush. You will find that a dry brush is easy to control, and "mistakes" will not be noticeable.

Step 6: Creating Detail

Unless you plan to put this piece of furniture in a very prominent place in your home, very little else need be done to create the appearance of grain. If, however, you are attempting to create the look of a special wood, you may want to enhance parts of the graining with fine detailing. Do this with a very fine artist's brush. Apply the paint in fine, thin lines to increase detail and define certain features.

Step 7: Protecting the Finish

Once the graining paint is thoroughly dry and has set for a day or two, apply a coat of clear varnish to protect the graining paint from wear. Acrylic paint is very durable, but it is not impervious to wear.

This pattern is then softened. A stiff vegetable brush was used to lighten the graining marks to make the pattern more natural. The brush is wiped clean after each stroke to avoid smearing.

A second coat of graining strokes is applied in a darker stain. This coat also is to be wiped and softened with a stiff brush before sealing.

SURFACE TEXTURING

If you have a table with a top that has been worn and abused to a point that seems beyond repair, creating a new surface may be the only answer. If the table is only a utility table and is never seen by visitors, you can probably cover the top with a sheet of quarter-inch plywood and paint that. However, if the table is otherwise attractive and useful, you may restore the top with craft plaster or gesso.

This material can be applied and smoothed to an even surface and then sealed and painted, or you can use it to create the impression of another type of surface. A smooth surface can be troweled on, sanded smooth, given a basecoat, with some mottling and individual grain lines to simulate marble. Then give the top a coat of high-gloss varnish.

A plaster surface may be applied to wood to create interesting textures and patterns, hide serious blemishes or poorly made repairs. The tools will determine the final texture.

Step 1: Mixing the Material

Purchase craft plaster, such as Craftex, at a paint store, craft shop or art supply store. This substance is sold as a powder to be mixed with water, and also is available premixed (but at high cost). Follow the directions on the label in order to mix the plaster material. Do not mix more than you can apply in a few minutes. The plaster will set up quickly and you do not want to have a bucket of dry, hard plaster as a doorstop when you finish.

Step 2: Applying the Plaster

Use a small trowel or wide putty knife to apply the plaster to the surface. You do not want to apply a thick coat. Fill in the worn and gouged spots first. Then create a level, smooth surface. If you want a smooth surface, apply a coating approximately 1/16 inch thick. If you want to create a simulated slate or travertine texture, you will have to apply a thicker coat, but avoid a coating deeper than ¼ inch or the edges of the plaster are likely to wear quickly.

Creating a Slate Texture Slate is layers of compressed rock. When it is cut, the layering sometimes shows in ridges.

To simulate a slate surface, apply and smooth the plaster. Use a knife to cut diagonally into the plaster and

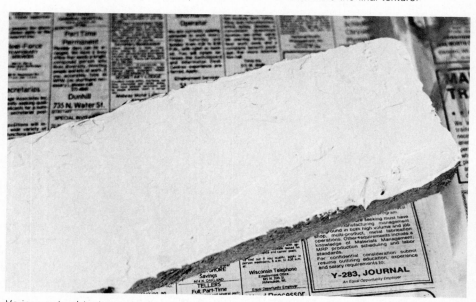

Various natural textures can be simulated with practice. When dry and painted, this might be an acceptable substitute visually for slate. Plaster will not be especially durable.

under the surface. Lift the blade of the knife slightly as you cut. Next, take a trowel and run it across the surface to flatten and slightly smooth the cuts. This will pull the edges of the cuts and create a surface similar to rough slate or flagstone.

Creating a Travertine Finish Travertine is the Swiss cheese of marble. The holes in the travertine are often in linear groups. Study a piece of the real thing before starting the project.

To create a travertine texture, use an awl or other pointed instrument to poke holes in the plaster surface.

Smooth the pitted surface as you work and remove plaster material as needed.

This surface is not suitable for a tabletop that is going to be exposed to moisture. Even with a coating of clear sealer, water would collect in the holes and eventually break down the sealer and the plaster.

Warning: Lack of Durability This plaster surface material will not last indefinitely under heavy use. Choose another finish if the piece of furniture, such as a desk, will receive constant use.

DECORATING WITH DECOUPAGE

This process applies printed material, photographs, art prints, and even—in some cases—photos from magazines, postcards or greeting cards.

Decoupage can be attractive decoration on ladderback chairs, chests and tables. The sealing process involves so many coats of varnish that the resulting finish is nearly impervious and has a glasslike surface.

THE OLD FASHIONED WAY
Step 1: Preparing the Printed Matter

Although it is possible to use a photograph from a magazine, material that is printed on both sides often has a "show-through" problem. When the decoration is coated with white glue to adhere it to the wood, the glue tends to cause the ink in the back to become visible on the face of the paper. To prevent this, coat the reverse side first with a very thin layer of white glue diluted to one-half strength. Let this dry overnight before beginning the decoupage process.

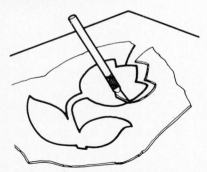

After you have chosen the printed material you want on your furniture, cut it away carefully with a sharp-pointed craft knife.

If the picture is on thick paper, you will have to soak some of the layers of the paper off the back. Coat the face with thinned varnish and let it dry thoroughly. Soak the paper in lukewarm water and lift as much of the paper off as possible without destroying the picture. For thick paper, remember that you will have to apply extra layers of varnish to bring the finished surface to a flat, level plane.

You may use a sharp knife or razor blade to cut precisely around the outline of the picture. However, other edge treatments are attractive. If the paper is relatively soft and fiberous,

gently tear the edges. Do not rip a whole side at a time; pull off small sections of the paper, separately in bits and pieces, to create a ragged edge that frames the picture. Parchment-style paper is often applied after the edges have been torn and furned. Very white paper can be rinsed in tea to give it a yellow and aged look. Let the sheet dry before handling.

Step 2: Preparing the Wood

Decoupage can be applied to new wood, stripped wood or finished wood. Sand the surface lightly to create a smooth surface. Fill any cracks, scratches or gouges. High-gloss finishes should be sanded with a fine sandpaper so the glue can grip the surface, but the finish should still feel smooth to the touch.

Step 3: Applying the Design

Place the picture on the wood and lightly mark the desired position onto the wood with a pencil.

Spread a piece of plastic or plastic wrap and lay the picture face down on the plastic. Spread full-strength white glue on the back, using your finger or a small brush. Bring the glue as close to the edge as possible.

Transfer the picture to the wood, placing it face up within the marked position. Cover the picture with a new piece of plastic and use a roller to press the picture flat. Work from the center toward the edges. Wipe away any glue that oozes out from under the picture. Use another, clean piece

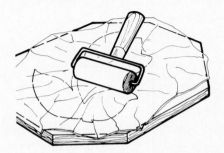

Apply white glue to the back of the printed matter, set into place and roll flat. Place waxed paper between pattern and roller.

of plastic over the picture and repeat this smoothing process until no glue seeps out. Wipe the wood clean of glue. White glue is water soluble; use

a slightly damp cloth to wipe the wood. Avoid touching the picture.

Step 4: Applying the Varnish

Wait twenty-four hours before starting to varnish. Check the picture for air bubbles. If you missed any, you will have to repair the bubble in the same way you repair a bubble in veneer: slit the surface above the bubble and, using a very fine probe—a wire or half a toothpick—apply white glue to the underside. Then smooth and flatten the bubble.

Apply varnish, either regular or polyurethane, to the entire surface. Let dry at least 24 hours, sand with fine, wet sandpaper, wipe the surface absolutely clean, and apply another coat of varnish. This process is repeated until the finish is level and the depth sufficient to protect the design and the wood. This could require as little as six or as many as twenty coats.

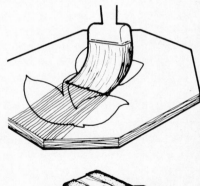

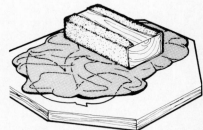

Coat the surface with varnish, let dry and then wet sand. Do this repeatedly until the surface is smooth and level and well protected.

QUICK-KIT DECOUPAGE

If all of this seems to be too long and difficult a process, there are kits that allow application and sealing of the surface in one or two operations. Although the surface will not resist wear as well as the many layers of varnish, the decoupage kit provides good protection for a surface that will not receive abuse or constant use.

STENCILING YOUR FURNITURE

This process, which involves applying paint through a mask, is a popular traditional American paint finish. You can work out a stencil as simple as a series of letter forms, useful for identifying whose chair is whose in a child's room; at the other extreme, you can reproduce elaborate wallpaper patterns and other decorative designs.

The Principles of Stenciling

To stencil, you apply a design with a paint through cutouts in a piece of plastic or waxed cardboard. The action of applying the paint is a dabbing, straight up-and-down motion. The proper brushes are short-bristled, thick and short-handled. The paint should be a fast drying, lacquer type. Beginners often attempt to stencil by applying the paint with a regular brush in a back-and-forth motion. This usually means that the edges of the design are not covered well. When the beginner discovers this, he or she then tends to over-apply the paint, stroking the ends of the bristles against the edges of the cutout. This usually leads to blotchy, thick coverage and bleeding of paint under the stencil.

APPLICATION PROCEDURES

Step 1: Choosing a Pattern

Commercially designed and manufactured stencils are available at many paint stores and craft shops. Designs range from simple to intricate; samples of the effect of the stencil are commonly on hand at the store. An intricate stencil pattern may be the product of combining as many as twelve masks to achieve the final result. An intricate stencil pattern will often look very much like a free-hand design if used only once (single motif).

If you have never tried stenciling, we suggest a simple, one- or two-mask stencil pattern. This will reduce the amount of time spent at the project and enable you to see the results faster.

Creating your own Pattern Individualized stencil patterns can be created by anyone. Sketch your design on paper and do a cutout test on thin paper to see how well the design holds together. Use a soft pencil or charcoal

A stencil pattern may brighten a plain box. While many stencil patterns are simple like this one, other may use multiple masks and be very complex and look like freehand painting.

Stencils may be cut from coated stencil board or light-weight Mylar. Use a very sharp, pointed knife so all edges are even and clean.

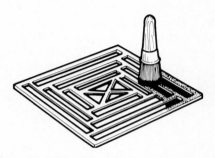

Use a stencil brush to apply the paint. A straight, up-and-down motion is best and least likely to force paint under the stencil.

to fill in the pattern. This will give you an idea of how the stencil will look. When you are satisfied with the result, cut out the stencil mask. Look for stencil board at craft shops and art supply stores.

Try to avoid patterns that require most of the mask to be cut away in fine lines. If you feel this design is necessary, use two masks, with one section duplicated so you can keep the pattern aligned, and create the pattern in a two- or three-step process. Cut exact duplicates of all your stencils so that you do not have to wait for one stencil pattern to dry before moving the mask to apply another pattern.

Step 2: Producing the Pattern

The quick-drying lacquer paints that are best for stencils are available in art supply and craft stores. These work well because they are formu-

lated to dry quickly and not spread under the edges of the stencil. However, if you cannot find the right paint, you can use other materials such as acrylic art colors.

Mark the location of the design on the piece of furniture. If it is to be centered, check the measurements carefully before starting. Tape the stencil pattern in place. Dip your stencil brush in the paint and touch the brush to a piece of paper to remove excess. Move the brush straight up and down to fill in the stencil. It is better to apply the paint lightly and to go over the stencil several times than to load the brush with paint.

Do not remove the stencil until the paint is dry. Then remove the tape and lift the stencil straight up. If any paint accumulates on the edges of the design or on the underside, clean it off or discard the stencil.

Step 3: Sealing the Design

When you have finished all the design patterns and they are dry, use a varnish to seal the surface.

Step 4: Detailing the Design

If you feel that the flat color of the stenciled pattern is not as attractive as you like, you can outline or shade parts of the design. Use a fine brush and work carefully. First practice on a design that has been reproduced on a piece of paper or scrap lumber.

HAND PAINTING

If you have an artistic flare and a high level of skill, you can free-hand paint a design on your furniture. There are many folk art traditions to draw upon, such as the Norwegian technique of Rosemaling.

To do a design free-hand, however, requires planning and preparation. Test your design on paper before attempting it on wood. Make sure the design is in scale with the piece of furniture and appropriate to the style.

If you are capable of hand painting, you will also have enough experience to choose your materials. Acrylic paints are a good choice because of their durability and ease of use.

Trompe l'Oeil Painting

A very skillful painter can create an entirely new facade on a piece of furniture or a wall through carefully executed painting. By choosing a single point as a "light source" and painting in highlight and shadow consistent with the indicated direction of light, a skillful painter can create the impression of a three-dimensional surface on a flat plane. In this fashion, it is possible to create the impression of carving or turnings in flat wood. Plain square drawers can become curved and carved.

The skill to do trompe l'oeil is not within the reach of everyone. However, practice may improve skills to a point where you can create the impression of a groove cut into the surface of a tabletop. This calls for painting a fine line and then adding a highlight line to one side and a shadow line to the other.

Plan your pattern layout and provide guidelines. Work will go faster if you have several stencils and do not have to wait for paint to dry before starting the next pattern.

A skillful person may use a free-hand technique to paint a pattern on furniture. This secretary has been decorated with flowers drawn in the same style as used in the room fabric.

7

Finishing, Repairing, Refinishing

When a writer we know worked as a housepainter, nothing surprised him more than the new look a freshly sanded and finished floor could give to a room. After days of the confusion and mess of being covered with drop cloths and dust, the sanding and then the shellacking of the floors gave a gleaming beauty.

The same effect, you will find, will be possible in your own home, whether you are painting and redoing the entire room or just the floor. As time passes any floor darkens, gets a little scratched, or otherwise suffers the abuse that comes with constant use. No interim maintenance or care can give the fresh, new look of a refinishing job.

This chapter will show you how to renew a floor that has seen better days. This process begins with repairs of any problems that may exist in the floor up through and including the maintenance of the new finish.

Before attempting any repairs, however, you should understand how floors are constructed. Once you understand the construction, most repairs will be simple. Even those repairs that are complicated will be easier to handle, because the process of repair will become comprehensible.

ANATOMY OF YOUR FLOOR

The supporting framework of the floor is made up of joists; first floor joists rest on the top of the foundation walls. Normally, joists are set sixteen inches on center; that is, there is a distance of sixteen inches from the center of one joist to the center of the next. Currently, many local codes dictate that the minimum size for joists be 2x6 stock; but, because codes vary, you may find that

A well-laid, natural wood floor is an asset to a room if it is attractive, nicely finished and well maintained. When it becomes worn, it can be renewed and given a fresh, durable finish.

Joists serve to support the floor above and to provide structural strength. They are evenly spaced 2x stock, usually with extra bracing.

your home has joists of 2x8, 2x10, 2x12. If your home is very old, you might even find 2x14 stock with the joists set closer than sixteen inches.

Helping to support the joists for the first floor is a girder that runs the length of the house and is itself supported by posts called lally columns.

Subfloor Construction

On top of the joists is the subfloor, which may be either sections of plywood or lipped, tongue and groove boards. The subfloor is nailed to the joists; the finish (visible) flooring goes over the subflooring.

PROBLEMS WITH FLOORS

Any number of problems can develop in a floor over a period of time. Some of the potential problems include: loose boards in the finish flooring; gaps between the subfloor and the joists; or improper nailing in the original work that must be corrected. Any problems of this nature must be eliminated before you begin to refinish a wood floor.

OVERVIEW OF THE REFINISHING PROCESS

Refinishing a floor requires a number

of steps. The process may seem difficult and time consuming as you consider it, but the work is largely done by machine at the beginning. A floor sander can strip an old finish from a floor and create a completely smooth, fresh surface in a matter of two or three hours.

After the floor has been stripped, you may want to stain the flooring, which means you may need to fill the pores of the wood and apply a clear sealer that protects the stain. Another alternative is to apply the final finish directly over the freshly sanded wood. The usual choices for a final finish are shellac, varnish and urethane varnish.

PARTIAL REFINISHING

In some cases, the basic finish of the floor needs a little touch up before a new coat of shellac or varnish is applied. This may require some touch-up sanding, the removal of heelmarks, and small repairs.

Maintaining The Floor Finish

Any floor, like any wood surface, requires a certain amount of maintenance. There are, however, some finishes that may not need wax. Consider the maintenance requirements before choosing and applying the finish.

Although board floors are most common, parquet, blocks of wood tile, is another natural wood flooring. It is usually prefinished.

REPAIRING THE FLOOR

The most common problem that occurs in a floor is that one or more spots in the floor squeak when walked on. The squeak is annoying, and that is reason enough for you to make a repair. However, the squeak usually also indicates that one or more of the components in the floor is loose.

Except for the first floor/basement ceiling, you probably will have to correct the problem from the top side of the floor only; there is seldom easy access from the underside. The underside of the floor will be finished by the ceiling of the room below. However, most problems can be solved from the exposed side.

LOOSE FLOOR BOARDS

Probably the most common problem occurs when one or two of the floor boards becomes loose. You can determine if this is the problem by stepping on the boards to discover exactly where the squeak is. Then apply a little pressure with your hand; you should be able to feel the boards moving. Once you have located the loose boards, drive a 2½ inch (8d) finishing nail into each board at the point where it is loose. This should drive the floor and subfloor more tightly together, eliminating the source of the squeak.

After you have driven in the one nail, step on the board. If there is still an audible squeak, drive a second nail into the board, placing it an inch or so from the first nail. After the nails have been driven in and the squeak eliminated, use a nailset and hammer to drive the nailheads slightly below the surface. Fill the hole with wood putty that comes as close as possible to the color of the finished floor.

GAPS BETWEEN SUBFLOOR AND JOISTS

Squeaks sometimes occur because the subfloor and flooring do not set firmly on a joist. If there is a slight gap, the subfloor will flex and rub against the joist when someone steps on the floor. The best solution is to fill the gap. If the framework is exposed, drive a thin, wedge-shaped piece of wood between the subfloor and the joist.

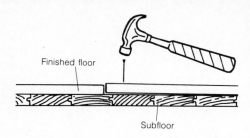

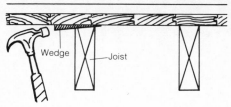

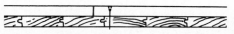

If flooring has come free of the subflooring, drive and countersink a fine finishing nail to reattach the finished flooring.

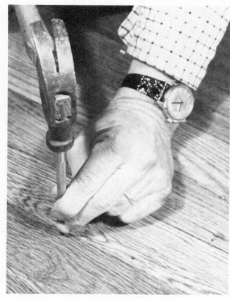

Use a nail set to countersink the finishing nail. This will allow you to hide the repair and make the new finish smooth.

Use a wood putty or other filler to cover the nail holes. Use a flexible knife to force the filler into the hole. Remove excess.

If subflooring flexes on the joists, try to drive a small wedge between the joist and subflooring. This should stop any squeaking.

A wood shingle is a good wedge because of its precut shape. Trim a shingle to size and drive the shingle/wedge into position.

If the joists are hidden, such as between a ceiling and upper floor, you will have to drive a nail through the finish flooring.

If you cannot do this without ripping out the ceiling below, you will have to attempt to correct the problem by nailing through the flooring and subflooring into the joist. Use a larger finishing nail for this than you used to secure the loose floor boards; a 10d or 12d nail will penetrate the top flooring and the subflooring and extend into the joist.

There will be some guesswork involved here because you will not be able to see the joists. Check the direction of the joists in your basement; measure the distance from center to center. Unless there is a drastic difference between the size and configuration of your first and second floors, this should help you to approximate the location of the joist. Drive the nails into the floor and on into the joist. If you miss the joist, you could create a new and possibly worse problem, which is discussed next.

NAILS RUBBING ON JOISTS
Squeaks can be caused by a nail driven through the subfloor but not into the joist, so that the nail presses against the side of the floor member. When someone steps on this spot, the floor deflects slightly and the nail rubs against the side of the joist. The solution is to drive additional nails through the finish floor and subfloor, down into the joists to hold the layers more firmly together.

REPAIRING PARQUET FLOORING
Parquet flooring also may be subject to squeaking. The parquet tiles may become loose and lift a bit; every time someone steps on the loose section, it will squeak. To solve the problem, drive small finishing nails into the raised portions of the tiles. However, if a tile is warped, this procedure may crack the tile. If this happens, secure the separate sections to the subfloor; countersink and fill the nailheads and the crack with appropriately colored putty.

SILENCING MINOR SQUEAKS
Occasionally, a section of flooring will squeak because the wood has dried just enough that the tongue-and-groove joints have shrunk a very little bit. When someone walks across the floor, the boards shift slightly and squeak. To eliminate this squeak, you may find that squirting a small amount of graphite powder into the tiny crack between the floor boards will provide sufficient lubrication to stop the sound.

Parquet flooring can squeak if it becomes loose. Use a fine nail to resecure the section to the subfloor. Countersink and fill the nail hole.

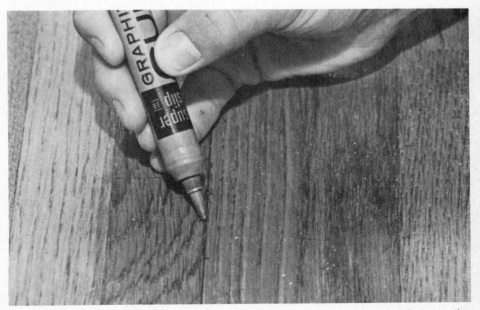

Some squeaks can be stopped by applying graphite powder in the small spaces between the flooring. Th lubrication will allow wood to move quietly.

REMOVING THE FLOOR FINISH

Although professionals sometimes neglect to wear a dust mask, we strongly recommend that all do-it-yourselfers take advantage of this protection. There is no reason to breathe irritating (and for some people, health-endangering) dust when you can buy inexpensive protective masks. These masks are sold in paint and hardware stores.

You also should wear goggles or safety glasses, especially if you wear contact lenses. Although the large sander has a vacuum bag and should control much of the dust, the small sander may not have this feature. You will be working on your hands and knees while using the small sander, and your face will be very close to the unit.

Being cautious with your health and safety can protect you from needless injury due to carelessness and "shortcuts."

Step 1: Repairing and Cleaning the Floor

Before beginning to refinish the floor, it is a good idea to check the entire surface for exposed nailheads or raised corners of boards. Either of these can rip to shreds a rapidly moving sandpaper belt. Clean the floor of chewing gum or other material that may have adhered to the surface; any gummy or sticky material will clog your sandpaper quickly. If the floor has holes, nicks or dents, fill these with appropriately colored putty.

One of the most difficult refinishing jobs is restoring a floor after you have removed a layer of linoleum or glued-in-place vinyl flooring. Some refinishers advise softening the mastic by running an iron over brown paper and then scraping off the softened mass.

Step 2: Removing Baseboards

Although it is not absolutely necessary, you may want to remove the baseboards. If the baseboards need repair and refinishing, you will find the work easier if the baseboards are off the wall. Pry the baseboards off carefully; this molding is fragile and breaks easily.

Use a stiff putty knife or a screwdriver with a thin blade. Start at an outside corner and carefully slip the blade between the molding and the wall. Place a thin piece of wood between the prying tool and the wall. This will provide better leverage and protect the wall surface from dents and other damage. Use light pressure to pry outward very gently. Then move an inch or so away from the point where you just worked and pry again. Repeat. As you pry, the nails that hold the molding in place will begin to pull free. Continue in this fashion, prying

Before sanding the floor, clean up any material stuck to the floor such as chewing gum. Anything sticky will clog the sandpaper.

When refinishing a floor, always remove as much of the base molding as possible. The closer you can get power sanding equipment to the wall, the easier and faster the job will be.

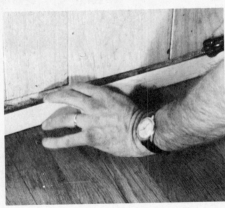

Use a screwdriver or small pry bar to release the molding from the wall. Pry gently every inch or two so you will not crack molding.

at one-inch intervals so that you do not bend and possibly break the molding. Eventually, it will pull free from the wall.

Do not exert extra pressure against the molding to speed the process; the baseboard will only break. You may then find you cannot match the molding and must purchase all new baseboard for your room.

If you seem to be having problems getting the nails to pull free, go back three or four inches and pry where you previously worked. Move along the molding and pry again. The repeated, gentle prying will release the nails.

Step 3: Obtaining the Proper Equipment

Floor sanding equipment is usually rented, and you should not have any difficulty in obtaining a unit at your local rental store. However, make a reservation for the date(s) you want to use it; floor sanders are popular equipment items.

The unit you will be supplied with is a drum sander, which has rollers that revolve the sandpaper at high speed. It should come with a disc or orbital hand sander for working on the perimeter of the room. All the sandpaper you will require for the job should be part of the rental price—the sandpaper will include coarse, medium and fine grades. Any unused and undamaged sandpaper can be returned for credit.

You also will require a hand scraper for removing the finish in the deepest corners of the room and a vacuum for

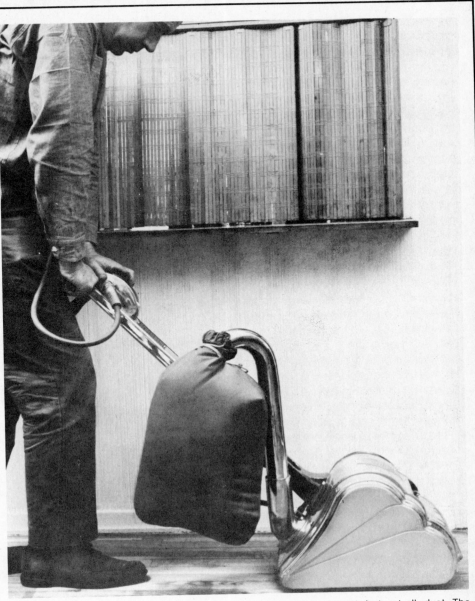

A power sander will come with a large dust bag that will control most, but not all, dust. The heavy equipment will make the stripping time relatively short and the job relatively simple.

taking up sanding dust. There is a vacuum bag on the sander but this does not do a thorough job. The floor also may require filling, and you may wish to stain it. Have these materials ready. These steps will be discussed in more detail later.

Step 4: Clearing the Room

Before beginning the sanding process, seal all electrical outlets and switches and all heating ducts and cold air returns. Use duct tape and heavy plastic sheets to cover the openings. Any dust that gets into the electrical or heating system can ignite explosively.

As an additional safety precaution, hang heavy drop sheets on either side of any door leading into the area in which you will be sanding. This will help to keep the dust created by the sanding within that area.

Remove everything from the room in which you will work. Take out all furniture, rugs and carpeting, all draperies, all curtains, window shades, as well as anything that hangs on the walls or is in built-in bookcases and/or cupboards.

Not only will it be easier to work in a completely empty room, but anything left in the room would be exposed to damage from the dust and grit produced during the sanding work.

As you work, you will have to remove the dust between sandings and scrupulously clean all surfaces before refinishing. Extraneous objects in the room will merely collect dust that must be removed. If you leave fabric-covered objects, such as upholstered furniture or drapes in a room, the dust that the sanding produces will get into and between the fibers. This will be very difficult to clean and may damage the material.

Step 5: Sanding The Floor

Your rental dealer should provide you with full instructions on how to install the sanding belts and how to operate the machine. If he does not, be sure to ask him for full instructions, which will vary from machine to machine.

The sander is a big, heavy machine with small metal rollers on which to wheel it when not in use. The sanding belt is one piece and slips over the rollers from one side. The belt is held in place by the pressure of the rollers. In use, the machine is pushed in one direction rather like a lawnmower. There is an on-off switch in the handle.

Rough Sanding Start in one corner of the room and work diagonally so that you push the sander at an approximately 45 degree angle to the length of the flooring. This will eliminate any irregularities on the edges or joints of the floor planks. Tilt the machine on the roller wheels so the sandpaper belt is NOT in contact with the floor and turn on the machine. Push the machine forward, gradually lowering the machine so that the sandpaper belt makes contact with the floor. *Never start the machine with the sandpaper belt touching the floor. Never stop moving the machine when the sandpaper belt is in contact with the floor.* Push the machine to opposite your starting point. As you reach the other side of the room, tilt the machine back and lift the sandpaper belt off the floor. If you stop or leave the belt in contact with the floor for any time in one spot, you will gouge the floor. This will leave marks that are nearly impossible to remove short of total resanding.

If you run the sander diagonally across the floor during the first sanding, you will smooth out unevenness. This sanding is taking off heavy material and is moving with the boards.

A small but powerful sander will be provided to sand the perimeter of the room. This will allow you to sand off the finish in all but the very corners and edge of the floor.

A hand scraper will be needed to remove the finish from the extreme corners and edges. This tool should be provided with the power equipment and is designed for this specific job.

Overlapping the sanded strips Move the machine as close to the wall opposite your starting place as you can without touching the wall. Tilt the handle of the machine down to lift the belt off the floor and pull the sander back to your starting point. Resand the same strip until all the finish has been removed. If there is only a single coat of finish on the floor, you may have to go over the strip only once. If there are many layers, you may have to resand two or three times. When the strip is free of finish, roll the machine to an adjacent area and position it so the belt will overlap the first strip by approximately three inches.

Repeat this procedure until you have sanded the entire floor and have taken off all the finish. Remember to move the machine slowly but steadily and never stop when the sanding belt is in contact with the floor.

Sand the border of the room When you have finished with this first rough machine sanding, you still will have a perimeter of unsanded area. Use the hand-held disc sander to remove the finish in this area. Move the hand sander back and forth from left to right. You will have to hold this unit tightly because it will want to "run away". For this first sanding, use coarse sandpaper, just as you did with the drum sander.

You will be able to do all of the border of the room with the disc sander, except for the absolute corners. To clear the corners, use the hand scraper to scrape the finish off. A small block of wood with a strip of sandpaper wrapped around it also is useful for working in corners. These two tools also will help you remove the floor finish in areas under radiators or other places where the disc sander cannot reach.

Cleaning up It should take approx- imately one-half hour to rough sand a 12x15 foot room. When the first, rough sanding has been completed, use a broom and vacuum to clean up as much of the sanding dust as possible. Any dust left will clog the next grade of paper as you work, and grit may scratch the floor surface. It is a good idea to wear soft, cotton socks on your feet as you sweep so there is no chance of grinding any of the dust into the floor with your shoes.

Medium Sanding Load the machine with medium sandpaper and repeat the procedure in exactly the same way you did the rough sanding except that this time you will sand from one end of the room to the other. It is vitally important to remember that the sanding machine should always be moving when it comes in contact with the floor. When the main area of the floor has been sanded, use the disc sander, loaded with medium paper, to do the borders of the room. Use the scraper and block of wood wrapped in sandpaper to do corners and other places the machines cannot reach, as you did the first time.

When you have finished the medium sanding, sweep and vacuum up all dust again. Be sure to wipe away dust that has settled on the tops of window and door frames and on window sills and the top edges of molding. The room should be as dust-free as possible when you plan to apply the final finish. Any dust that settles on the wet shellac or varnish will cause problems.

Fine Sanding Finish the sanding with the fine sandpaper. The medium sanding should have made the floor very smooth; the fine sanding stage will make it nearly silky smooth, so that the final finish application will be absolutely even. Follow the same sanding procedures used previously. Sand in overlapping strips, following the direction of the boards and always keeping the machine moving. Sand the main area first, then the borders and then the corners. Sweep and vacuum up the dust. Wipe down the walls and ceiling and finish by wiping with a tack rag, especially in corners and under obstructions such as radiators.

STAINING WOOD FLOORS

Many years ago, shellac or varnish was considered sufficient finish on a floor. Today, however, many people stain floors for the same reason they stain wood furniture. Staining brings out the beauty of the wood or adds a beauty to a wood that does not have it naturally.

Step 1: Choosing and Testing the Stain

Stain should be applied immediately after completion of the fine sanding and after all the dust has been removed with a vacuum, a broom and a tack rag. One can choose among various types for a floor, but it is important to select a stain that is compatible with the final finish material. Check the label before making your selection. Consider the effect of the stain on the wood, too. For example, one stain is a pigmented material that wipes on and colors the wood like paint. While this is easy to apply, the stain tends to be opaque and hides the grain pattern of the wood. Try out any stain in an inconspicuous area before applying to the entire floor. The ideal test area is the floor of a closet. The next best choice for a test area is a spot on the floor that will be covered by a rug or hidden by furniture.

Step 2: Applying the Stain

Apply stain to your test area; let it set. Then wipe off the stain with a clean, dry cloth. Repeat the procedure at increasing intervals so you can judge how long it should stand on the floor. Once you have settled on a setting time for the stain, use a brush to apply the stain, keeping the overlapping brush strokes to a minimum. Let the stain seep into the wood. Wipe away the excess with clean, dry cloths. Plan the application of the stain so that you are always working in a dry area. The worker who paints or stains himself or herself into a corner is more common than you may think.

Allow the stain to dry for at least twenty-four hours before applying filler or a clear finish coat.

Variation: Using Special Stains

Type 1: Non-grain Raising Stain

Like its counterpart for furniture, a non-grain raising stain for floors will not lift the grain of the wood. This means that tiny, hairlike filaments of wood do not come up on the surface of the boards to create a relatively rough finish. This staining feature saves time and effort because additional sanding is not required after staining. Non-grain raising stain comes in a wide variety of colors; however, it is an expensive material. Also, it is difficult to apply evenly.

Type 2: Penetrating Oil Stain

This stain also has the advantage of not raising the grain, but it has a significant disadvantage: the stain tends to mix with filler, varnish or shellac applied later. Regular non-grain raising stain does not do this. To avoid the problem of this stain mixing with final finish materials, apply a coat of thin (1 pound cut) shellac to the stained surface before applying the other final finishing coats.

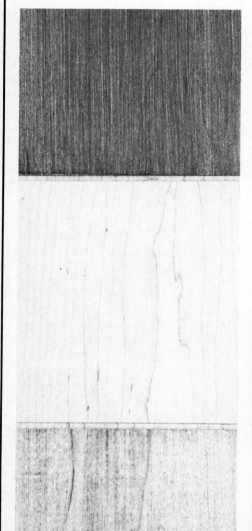

If you stain your floors, choose a color and type to bring out the quality you want most. Some stains bring out grain; others hide it.

Plan your staining so that you can apply, let stand, and wipe off the stain to get the effect you want. Do not do too much at once. Do not work into a corner you cannot escape.

FILLING AND FINISHING THE FLOOR

Some open-pore woods, such as oak, walnut and mahogany require filling before any final finish is applied. Otherwise, finish can seep into pores and create a very uneven appearance. If your floor is oak, you will probably have to fill the newly sanded surface. Some older homes have maple floors; maple is a close-grain wood and does not need to be filled.

Step 1: Applying the Filler

Obtain paste filler and thin it as needed with turpentine, following the label directions. One of the most effective methods is to apply filler with steel wool. Rub against the grain to force the filler into the pores of the wood. Fillers are available both neutral and colored. You can also add color to filler if you wish to match your floor.

Rub the filler on the floor and apply the compound to as much of the floor as you can at one time. After it has set for a half hour, rub it in so the filler is forced into the pores. Before the filler dries, remove the excess with a rag moistened with turpentine. If you do not remove the excess, it will bleed through your final finish.

Step 2: Choosing The Right Finish

When all the dust has been wiped from all the surface in the room—including the walls and ceiling, you can apply the final finish. There are many alternatives available. The most common are shellac, varnish and polyurethane varnish. However, if the wood is particularly beautiful and the room does not receive heavy foot traffic, you may want to use a penetrating oil finish.

Shellac This used to be the standard floor finish, but it has not been used as much in recent years. Although it provides a strong finish, it is susceptible to damage from liquids. In fact, if it is applied when the humidity is high, it may dry with a clouded finish.

The shellac you use for a floor is the same as you use for furniture. The choices include white shellac, which is clear, and orange shellac, which is amber-colored. Most people prefer the white shellac. Make sure you purchase real shellac and not a substi-

Oak is an open-grain wood. Oak flooring should be filled if you want to have a completely smooth finish on the floor. Apply the filler according to the directions on the container.

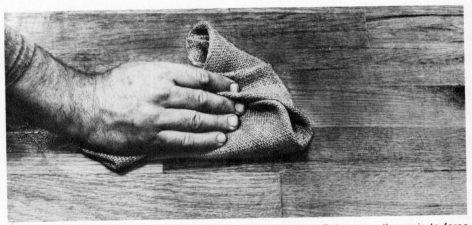

Steel wool or burlap will force filler into the pores of the wood. Rub across the grain to force the filler in; rub with the grain to remove any excess on the surface of the wood.

tute, imitation material. The substitutes are seldom as durable or scratch resistant when given the wear a floor will receive.

The most attractive feature of shellac is the ease with which it is applied with a brush. Another advantage is its quick drying time, which allows you to lay two coats, or even three, in a single day.

Varnish This material has been a standard wood finish for many years. It creates a hard, durable finish. In relatively recent years, however, addition of polyurethanes to the varnish has changed the formulas and increased the range and suitability of the varnishes available for floors.

There are various characteristics to varnish, and you have to make several decisions when you choose the finish. Varnish comes in high or medium gloss or a flat finish. There are both slow-drying and relatively quick-drying varnishes. However, the latter are not

nearly as quick-drying as shellac, nor are they usually as durable as the slow-drying types. One of the tougher varnishes is spar varnish, which is favored by many professionals. It dries very slowly and has a medium gloss. Because it dries slowly, you may find the waiting time between coats so long that your home remains in confusion over too long a period, making it difficult for your family to cope.

There are varnishes manufactured in formulas designed especially for use on floors; these are specifically labeled as such. Shop carefully for the best choice for your home.

Polyurethane Varnishes Polyurethanes are another family of varnish floor finishes and these also are favored by many professional floor refinishers. The first of these was Fabulon, but now there are a number of different polyurethane finishes marketed now. The urethane added to the varnish increases the durability of the

Project continued on next page

surface. In general, the more polyurethanes in the varnish, the better the finish.

Application of polyurethane varnishes may be made with either a brush or a roller.

Penetrating Oil Finishes Under certain circumstances, penetrating oil finishes may be used on floors. This is exactly the same material used on furniture. Penetrating oil finishes come clear or colored; you may change or enhance the color of the floor as you apply the finish.

Step 3: Applying The Floor Finish

Shellac Because the shellac is the same material as used on furniture, apply shellac to the floor in exactly the same manner indicated for furniture (see Chapter 5 for in-depth discussion). Dip the brush in the shellac and let it flow from the brush onto the floor surface. Use a brush that is as wide as one or two of the boards and move the brush only in one direction. You may stop when you come to a joint between the ends of boards. Try to avoid overlapping your strokes from one board to another.

Between applying coats of shellac, rub the floor lightly with steel wool. Use three or four coats for good coverage and a more lasting surface.

Varnish Application of regular varnish to a floor follows the same steps as its application to furniture. Complete directions, however, will be printed on the can. Observe these directions scrupulously, especially if you are using a floor-type varnish.

Because varnish dries slowly, you have to be careful to keep dust from settling on the wet or sticky surface. However, minor imperfections in your brushwork can be stroked out if noticed early. If you miss a small spot, a second coat will usually flow into and hide the "mistake".

Allow at least twenty-four hours between coats; more time may be advisable. Spar varnish may require forty-eight or more hours to dry.

Sand lightly between coats and wipe the floor with a tack rag before applying a fresh coat.

Polyurethane Varnish This type of

A polyurethane varnish is a good choice for a floor that will receive very heavy use. Plan the finishing job and allow yourself plenty of time. Allow full drying time between coats.

varnish is more forgiving than regular varnish when it comes to application. One of the greatest advantages of this type of varnish is that it can be applied to floors with a roller, which simplifies the job considerably. However, no roller can complete the perimeter of the floor without touching the wall, so you first must use a brush to cover the floor around the room perimeter.

Penetrating Oil There is nothing simpler to apply than an oil finish. You can apply it with a brush, a roller or a rag. Let the oil penetrate into the surface and then wipe the surface dry with a soft, clean cloth. The wiping and rubbing gives the finish a warm sheen that is very pleasing. You may apply additional coats each twenty-four hours until the wood takes on the appearance you desire.

This finish is nearly impervious to moisture, but provides little protection from scratches. It is not a good choice in an area where children play with toys on the floor or for other areas that receive heavy use. However, the appearance can be incomparable in a formal room used mostly by adults.

TOUCH-UPS FOR FLOOR FINISHES

If your floors have not been sanded for some time, you do not need to assume that they necessarily must be completely refinished. If a floor has been varnished or polyurethaned and is in reasonably good condition, you only may need to touch it up; no removal of the old finish is required.

APPLYING A NEW FINISH OVER THE OLD

Step 1: Cleaning the Floor Finish

Use a paint cleaner to clean the floor thoroughly. Follow manufacturer's directions. Rinse off the cleaner, taking care to wipe the floor dry quickly. Any moisture left on the floor could damage the wood.

When the floor is dry, use fine steel wool to rub out heelmarks and other obvious mars; fine sandpaper also works well. If there are rough spots on the floor, use fine grade sandpaper to smooth the rough spots until they blend with the rest of the floor. Elim-

inate any rough edges that will mar a fresh varnish or other finish.

Vacuum the dust from the floor and wipe with a rag dampened with mineral spirits. You must remove all the dust. Finish wiping the floor with a tack rag.

Step 2: Adding A New Finish

Next, apply two coats of the same clear finish that is already on the floor.

Follow label directions for thinning and sanding between coats.

PROTECTING THE FINISH

Once your floor is finished to your satisfaction, it is a good idea to maintain it properly. This ensures greatest durability.

Shellac and Varnish Protection

These finishes will be enhanced and

All floor finishes will benefit from good maintenance and reasonable protection. A good paste wax application will help most floors.

A power buffer makes the polishing job easier and the finish more attractive. This is a job that takes time, but except for heavily trafficked areas, needs to be done only once a year.

Project continued on next page

Parquet requires the same protection and maintenance as any wood floor. It is designed for constant, heavy wear and will withstand continuous use as long as you keep it clean and polished.

Wood floors are the standard desired in fine homes. They are durable and retain their value. Photo reproduction and vinyl coating in this floor provide a simulation that substitutes for the real wood.

protected by wood floor wax. Depending upon the amount of traffic and wear given a floor, you may need to renew the wax every six months to a year. Clean the floor as directed by the manufacturer of the wax product you have chosen. A good paste wax will provide the most durable protection for your wood. Use an electric buffer to polish the finish.

Polyurethane Varnish Protection
The advantage of this material is that

it only needs damp mopping. Paste wax may be applied if you wish, but one of the advantages of urethane varnish is that the surface is durable and nearly impervious to harm.

Oil Finish Protection
The best protection for this finish is to wipe it regularly with a soft dust mop or a tack rag. Grit will scratch the finish so it is advisable to place a small rug at the threshold of a room. This means that those entering may have

a place to wipe off dust and dirt from their shoes.

If a scratch occurs, you can apply more of the oil finish to the spot and rub the area back to the luster of the rest of the floor.

8
Stripping Millwork, Molding, Paneling

The actual removal of the existing finish from moldings, millwork and paneling is no different from removing finishes from furniture. The variations, such as they are, develop when dealing with architectural features or details that must be stripped in place.

Whenever possible, remove the molding, door or window from its location and apply the stripper. This process is not always possible. You will probably find the prospect of dismantling a complete set of stair banisters and railing more awesome than the prospect of controlling the mess involved in stripping these pieces in place.

There is some millwork that can be removed temporarily from the usual locations and worked on more conveniently. Doors, windows and moldings can, as a general rule, be taken down, stripped, refinished and returned to their original positions. Paneling, full sets of banisters, and highly decorated fireplace surrounds, as a rule, cannot.

We will attempt to guide you through the processes involved in both situations.

Woodwork and built-in cabinets should be an asset to a home and should be refinished when they become worn or unsightly.

Banisters and other decorative woodwork are often difficult to refinish because of their style and permanent location. All adjacent surfaces must be protected from spattered stripper.

REMOVING DOORS, WINDOWS OR BUILT-INS

DOORS

Most doors are installed with loose-pin hinges that enable you to remove the door for painting or adjustment. You should wedge the door firmly so it will not slip or pull against the hinge-plate screws as you work. If the door is large and heavy, find someone to help you to remove the door.

Extracting the Hinge Pin

The hinge pins fit through the meshed hinge loops. If the hinge is relatively loose, you may be able to remove the pin simply by grasping the small knob at the top and lifting the pin out. Years of wear and pulling, however, may have bent the pin so that it is jammed into the hinge. Use the end of a nail puller to pry the pin from the hinge.

If the pin is tightly wedged in the hinge, you may have to tap it out with a hammer. If this will not release the pin, you will have to remove the entire hinge.

Whenever possible, remove doors for stripping. Lay the door flat so the stripper will stay in place and work faster.

Remove the hinge pin to remove the door. Clean the pin while it is out so it can be replaced easily and work better.

Variation: Taking the Hinge Off If

the pin is damaged and will not come out, or if the hinge is a tight-pin hinge that does not allow pin removal, you will have to remove the entire hinge.

Open the door and wedge it securely. If possible, open the door all the way so that it touches a wall. Place a heavy weight against the door so that it cannot move.

Find a screwdriver with a tip that fits the plate screws. A screwdriver tip that is too small will shift and tear up the slot; a screwdriver tip that is too large will not fit and will slip and scratch the plate. Remove the hinges from the wall. There will be at least three screws in each plate and a minimum of two hinges for a door. Leave one screw part way in each plate until you have checked that the door is braced securely and will not slip when the final screws are released from the hinge plates.

Support the door well so that the weight of the door is not applied to the last screw and hinge as it is loosened. Exterior doors are particularly heavy. Find a willing and strong assistant to help you remove exterior doors.

Setting the Door Up for Finishing Work

Once the door has been removed, you can make any repairs and refinish as needed (described later in this chapter). Lay the door across two saw horses or on a large work table. Make sure the surface is flat and stable.

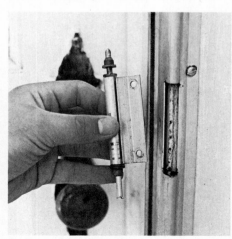

If the hinge pin is jammed or not meant to be removed, brace the door securely and remove the entire hinge from the door.

WINDOWS

Windows always pose a problem for the finisher/refinisher. It is very easy to paint them shut. Attempting to refinish a window in place may lead to a great many awkward and messy situations. If there is only one layer of finish on the window, you can probably strip it in place without difficulty, but if there are many layers, you would be advised to take the window out of the frame and work on the two elements separately.

Standard double-hung windows are often a problem to refinishers. However, it is possible to remove the sash from the frame.

Step 1: Removing the Stop Molding

An older window is held in place by stop molding. This type of window is controlled by weights. The window section with the glass weighs the same as the weight, so the unit is always in balance. If you raise the window, the weight is lowered. The balance between the two parts keeps the window open at the point you choose.

There is stop molding on the inside and the outside of the frame. You will be concerned with the inside stop molding. The molding is nailed to the frame and overlaps the space occupied by the window unit. To remove the window, pry off the molding.

Insert a thin-bladed knife under the edge of the molding; place a piece of folded cloth between the handle of the knife and the window frame. This will cushion the handle of the knife and protect the frame from scratching or denting. Lift very gently; this molding is delicate. Move the knife an inch and pry again. Try to get the molding to lift a little. Repeat the prying process from top to bottom several times so the nails are pulled free slowly and so no real pressure is applied to the molding. Eventually this will free the mold-ing. Repeat on the other side of the window.

Step 2: Pulling Out the Window

Once the molding is off, you can pull the window out of the frame. The unit will be attached to the weight by a chain or a piece of rope. For the mo-ment, tape the chain or rope to the frame with duct tape. Pull the window unit out of the frame. This should be easy to do; most older windows are loose. If it fits snugly, pull gently from the bottom. Once the window unit is out of the frame, unhook or untie the chain or rope from the window unit.

Step 3: Removing the Weights

Once the window section is out of the frame, you will see a small panel; this gives you access to the weights. The panel may be held by a pressure fit-ting, nails or screws. Remove the panel. Hold on to the rope or chain and release the tape. Lower the weight until the top can be reached through the access panel. Unhook or untie the weight and pull it through the panel. Pull the chain out of the hole at the top.

Variation: Newer Windows

Although all double-hung windows slide up and down in the frame, in newer windows the sections may be held in place with the constant pressure ap-plied by a strip of metal in the track. This metal strip looks similar to metal weatherstripping. This window will not have stop molding.

If your window has this metal spring strip in the track, you will be able to remove your windows quickly and easily. The window may be connected to a pully system with fine braided wire cable. If so, there will be a small notch in the metal strip. Slip the braided wire into the notch; this holds the wire in place. Lift the window while, at the same time, applying light pressure to the wire. This releases the wire from the movable window unit. Push the unit against one side of the frame while pulling the other side of the unit toward you. The entire glass/frame sliding unit will come out.

HANDLING BUILT-IN UNITS

Kitchen and bathroom cabinets, built-in bookcases, and other permanently installed units that require refinishing should be taken apart as much as possible. Remove the doors and all adjustable shelves. The more working room you can create in the interior, the easier it will be to remove the finish.

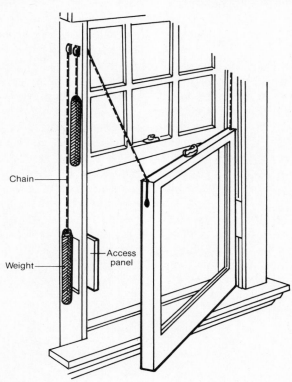

Chain

Weight

Access panel

After the stop molding has been carefully pried off the frame, the sections of sash may be pulled out of the frame. An access panel is useful when removing the sash weights.

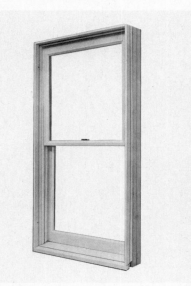

A modern, pressure-style sash is easier to re-move and replace. You do not have to worry about dropping the sash weights in the frame.

Some newer windows also flip down and lift out for easy removal. Obviously, refinishing chores are made simpler with these units.

STRIPPING THE FINISH

STEP 1: PROTECTING WORKING AREAS

Certain materials and types of wood architectural features simply cannot be removed for refinishing. Real wood paneling, banisters and handrails, ornate mantel pieces and/or fireplace surrounds could be irreparably damaged by attempted removal. Restoration to the original location also may be very difficult.

When removing an item from its location presents a greater problem than the actual stripping, your concern becomes protecting the areas around the feature to be stripped. Because stripper will remove a finish from almost anything it touches, you will have to protect the adjacent walls and floor.

Tape several thicknesses of newspaper to the walls. Three or four layers should be sufficient. Use masking or drafting tape to attach the paper to the walls. Change the paper regularly if it becomes wet from the stripper.

The finish on wood floors will be lifted by remover. This may not be a problem if you are planning to refinish the floor. However, other types of floors may be seriously damaged if stripper settles on the surface. Stripper will dissolve asphalt or rubber tile, linoleum, and eat into the finish of vinyl flooring. It will damage many plastic materials, synthetic fabrics used in carpeting and drapes, and even fiberglass. Use a drop cloth covered with newspapers to protect the floor. If possible, lift or roll back the carpeting.

STEP 2: APPLYING THE STRIPPER

Paint and varnish will require the use of a varnish remover. Use paste remover for all vertical surfaces. Application is easier to control and dripping or running is held to a minimum.

Apply the stripper on the wood work as you did to the furniture—in one direction only. Apply a thick coat, but do not use so much stripper that its own weight pulls it down the surface. If there are several layers to be removed, cover the stripper with a layer of newspaper to retard evaporation. Leave the stripper on the surface as long as possible without allowing the material to dry on the surface. Keep the windows open while you use the stripper; the fumes are toxic. Do not smoke in the room in which you are working. It is advisable to turn off the pilot lights to your stove, refrigerator, air conditioner, water heater and furnace if these appliances are gas powered. You do not want to run the risk of an explosion, or the possible conversion of the fumes to more toxic ones, by combining them with any flame.

STEP 3: REMOVING THE STRIPPER

The manufacturer of the stripper will indicate the time it should take to cut through the surface finish material. At the time suggested, check the progress of the stripping by wiping off a small area with a piece of steel wool or lifting the stripper off with a putty knife.

If the wood is clean under the stripper, follow the manufacturer's directions for removing and neutralizing the stripper. Clean the wood as suggested. (Reread Chapter 4 on removing furniture finish for more details.)

When you are working on a built-in cabinet, remove the finish from the inside, then the edges and any exposed sides. Use an orange stick with fine steel wool wrapped around the end to remove stripper in carved or turned areas. You may need to use a toothpick to dig the stripper out of fine grooves.

Work on one area at a time and try not to get stripper on an adjacent area. Use newspapers to protect areas to be stripped later. Stripper applied accidentally and allowed to dry will cause a discoloration of the wood.

If you are going to repaint wood that you are stripping, you do not have to be as particular, but if you are planning to use a new, clear finish, your wood must have an even, unspotted look.

In an older home the woodwork may have been finished with shellac. Test the finish with denatured alcohol to see if the surface dissolves before using a stronger stripper. If the alcohol dissolves the finish, it is shellac. Use the alcohol as your stripper.

Extra care must be taken when working around antique installations. Anyone refinishing the built-in cabinets that flank this fireplace must provide protection for the carved wood.

9

Repairing Wood in the Home

Just as furniture and floors need repairs before refinishing, so do molding, windows, doors and other wood items in the home. The first step is to examine the wood for any problems. Be very observant and never anticipate that a new coat of varnish will hide a problem that should be repaired. A new finish will usually make the problem more obvious. Problems fall into certain areas: those that occur in the wood surface, such as cracks that develop at joints or fasteners that come loose; structural problems in doors or windows; or such items as broken glass. Some problems resemble those common to wood furniture, but others require different solutions.

Fine, well-maintained woodwork is an asset to a home. Noticeable scratches, cracks and gouges will keep any woodwork from looking good and adding appeal to a room or a setting.

Age and dry air may alter the appearance of well installed paneling, cabinetry and woodwork. Regular inspection and care are needed.

Some materials, such as pre-finished wood paneling seem to be maintenance-free items, but they do need care. Regular cleaning is needed as well as checks of seams and nails.

REPAIRING MOLDINGS

Any woodwork, including doors and windows can become gouged and chipped. You can follow the same procedures to repair these problems that were discussed in Chapter 3 for repairing furniture.

HANDLING GOUGES AND GAPS

There are often gaps between structural members of windows and doors, caused by the expansion and contraction of the house. In time, molding dries and commonly separates at the mitre joints. These gaps should be filled and sanded smooth, or they will be very apparent when you apply the new finish. On windows, check the case molding miter joints and the joint between the stop molding and the side framework of the window. Check the equivalent joints on door facings and stop molding.

Base molding will dry as it ages and shrinks; this makes it pull away from the wall. This gap will show quite readily—especially if the wall and base molding are finished alike. Use a rubber mallet to tap the molding flush with the wall. If this does not work, you can pry the molding off the wall and reinstall it with slightly larger fasteners, or use a wood filler on the gap between the top of the molding and the wall. Choose a filler that is tinted to match the wood color if you are using a clear finish.

In some cases, molding will crack. Sometimes you can solve this problem by using brads to nail the molding sections together and close the crack. The brads used to secure the molding should have their heads countersunk and the depressions filled with wood putty. If the crack still shows, use filler to seal it. Sand the filler in the molding, as you would in furniture.

If you feel that wood filler will be too obvious when the finish is applied, another solution is to try to hide the repairs with the wood itself. Use a very small and narrow, sharp chisel to pry up a sliver of wood at the point you wish to drive a nail. Lift the sliver up and push the nail or brad into place. Drive it in with a small hammer and sink it with a nail set. Use white glue to adhere the sliver in place; hold the wood in position with a strip of masking tape until the glue sets. This technique takes skill and is tedious, but it will preserve the appearance of the wood grain.

PROTRUDING NAILS

If there are any nails or loose screws on the molding (or on doors and windows), hammer to reset or remove them and replace them with longer, larger nails. Replace any loose screws. Fill screw holes, if necessary, to provide a good bite for the screw thread. Check for nail holes; nails may sometimes work loose and have been pulled out. Fill holes with wood filler as needed.

A common problem is separation of mitre joints in molding. If the space is wide, it can be annoying to look at and a dust collector.

A crack wide enough to be noticed should be repaired. You may close the crack by nailing.

An easier solution is to fill the crack with putty or plaster and smooth over the space.

To make a hidden nail repair, lift a small sliver of wood with a sharp knife point. Make the sliver cut as small as you can.

Use as small a finishing nail as you can. Drive nail in the area under the sliver. Pull sliver to one side, but do not break it off.

Countersink the nail and apply white glue to the area. Press the sliver into place and let glue dry. Refinished repair will not show.

Replace protruding nail with larger one. If nail has worked out, drive new nail near the original location and fill any visible holes.

REPAIRING DOORS

LOOSE SCREWS

The most common reason a door sticks is that the hinge screws are loose. When this occurs, the door will sag and rub against the frame so that when closed, it is difficult to open—and when open, it is difficult to fit into the frame.

First tighten the screws. While it is normally the screws in the top hinge

that are loose because they take the most stress, it would not hurt to tighten all the screws. To insure that you can work without the door weight pulling against you, open the door and wedge a book or block of wood under the door.

You may find that the screwholes are so chewed up that you cannot tighten the screws. Remove the door;

follow directions given in the previous chapter. Fill the screwholes with plastic wood or slivers of wood coated with white glue; pack the material solidly into the holes. Let the filling dry, then install new screws a half inch longer than the ones you removed. The door should hold securely.

Because of the stress of opening and closing, hinge screws work loose. Check these regularly and tighten any that have worked loose.

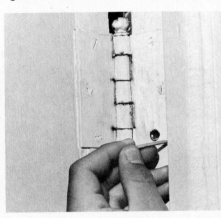

If the hole has become too large for the screw, fill with wood scraps and white glue. Let this set before reinstalling the screw.

PAINT BUILDUP

In some cases, the hinges will be secure but the door has become too fat to fit into its frame because of buildup of paint on the edge.

Use a chisel, a knife, or sandpaper to remove the buildup, and perhaps a little wood. Work gradually, frequently testing the door fit.

WEATHER CONDITIONS

In the summer, in regions with high humidity, the door may swell and become just a little too large for the frame. In this case, it is suggested that you lubricate the edge of the door with silicone spray before trying anything else. If it still does not fit in the frame, remove the lubrication and use sandpaper to take off a very little bit of wood until the door fits. Remember that the door will shrink in dry weather, so you do not want to make it too loose.

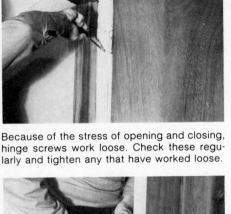

If a door sticks along one edge, you may be able to sand down a layer of paint to give the area enough clearance to move freely.

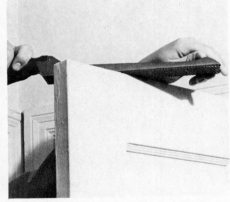

Weather changes or shifting of a structure may make the door too large for the frame. Plane or rasp off enough for the door to fit.

PROBLEMS IN THE FRAME

One other common reason for the door's not fitting properly is that the frame has sagged and is out of alignment. This usually occurs as a result of the natural settling of the house. The top member of the frame, the header that runs horizontally across the top of the door, may be perceptibly higher on one side than the other. One indication of this will be rub marks on the top (header) of the door frame.

If the misalignment is slight, the solution is to raise the frame just a bit so that the door can slide in easily. To do this, drive a 10d finishing nail up into the header where the door is sticking. This should bite into the structural framing and raise the header. More severe misalignment can mean that a serious structural problem exists. This should be evaluated by a structural engineer.

Molding separated from the frame may have to be secured by new nails driven in place.

REPAIR TO A LOOSE DOORKNOB

A loose doorknob can make it difficult to open and close a door properly. Sometimes it can make a door a trap rather than an exit. The solution to this problem is usually simple.

Look for a small screw on the neck of the knob on one side of the door. Use a thin-bladed screwdriver to loosen this screw, but do not remove it. Holding the knob on the other side of the door, rotate the knob with the screw all the way to the right as you push in, until the neck of the knob contacts the door plate. You may have to push quite hard to do this.

When the neck is flush against the plate, check the knob for operation. If it is too tight, the latch will get caught in the door and you will have further difficulties. If this is the case, rotate the knob a quarter turn to the left to loosen the latch. Now tighten the small set screw. The knob should work properly.

STRIKER PLATE REPAIRS

If a door does not close properly, it could be because the door does not fit into the frame; however, it also may be that the latch and striker plate are misaligned. If so, remove the striker plate (a couple of screws hold it) and use a file to slightly enlarge the opening so it can accept the latch.

If the latch does not fit far enough into the striker plate to hold the door closed, remove the plate and, using the plate as a pattern, cut a plywood shim to match. Quarter inch plywood should be thick enough. Cut a cardboard shim the same size as the latch to test the size and depth of the hole in the plywood and frame. Reinstall the striker plate over the plywood shim. Use new screws, long enough to hold the striker plate and the plywood shim firmly in the door casing.

Latch Maintenance

If the latch becomes stuck, frequently it is due to corrosion or simply to dirt accumulating and gumming the mechanism. Try squirting powdered graphite into the works through the lock mechanism. If this does not work, remove the doorknob and the screws that hold the latch mechanism in the door. Pull the unit out of the door. Clean and lubricate the latch pieces, and reinstall in the unit in the door.

CABINET DOORS

There are a number of cabinet catches, and any will create a problem if one or both parts become loose. One type of catch that often becomes loose and prevents a door shutting is the friction catch. A friction catch consists of a bent metal piece that is attached to the door, and a mating receptacle mounted on the edge of a shelf. Usually the problem is that, through repeated opening and closing, the parts become misaligned and do not mate. The solution is to realign the catch parts so that they do mate.

If you examine the shelf catch, you will see that it is held in place by a couple of tiny screws that go through a pair of slots (not holes). Loosen these screws a bit, reposition the catch, then try out the door. When the door does engage the catch, simply tighten the screws firmly.

Magnetic catches usually install the same way and can become similarly misaligned. Reposition them in the same way.

Set screw in the handle of a doorknob holds the knobs and the latch tongue. If knob needs adjustment, loosen, adjust and retighten.

Wear pattern on this striker plate shows that the latch tongue is lower than the hole. The plate should be moved down slightly to fit.

All hinges will wear and eventually bind if they are not lubricated regularly. A dry graphite lubricant is a good choice for hinges.

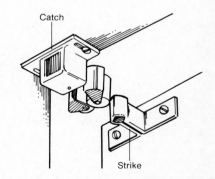

Because the catch on a friction or magnetic cabinet closure is adjustable, it may loosen and slip too far back to hold the strike.

REPAIRS TO WINDOWS

STUCK WINDOWS
The most frequently seen problem with windows is that they become stuck and will not open or close. The cure for the problem depends partially upon the type of window.

Double-hung Windows
The most common reason for a stuck window of this type is that paint has built up in the track of the window preventing it from sliding, or the window has been painted shut.

To free a painted-shut window, slip a thin-bladed knife between the window frame and the edge of the track, cutting the paint seal. You may have to do this both inside and out; windows can be painted shut from either side.

If you seem to have cut the seal but the window is still stuck, use a hammer and block of wood to vibrate the window and frame. Place the block of wood against various points around the frame and rap it sharply with the hammer. This shakes the window and, hopefully, breaks the paint seal.

Once the window has been freed, push it up and down several times, until it becomes easy to move. Then apply lubrication in the track. A silicone spray is best, but you can also use wax or paraffin. However, take care to keep the lubricant away from any window part that will be refinished. If necessary, clean off the surface with turpentine.

Slide-by Windows
Slide-by windows can become hard to budge because of soil accumulation in the track. Brushing the soil away will usually solve this problem. It is also an excellent idea to lubricate these windows regularly.

Casement Windows
Casement windows usually are the kind that are opened with a crank handle. As with double-hung windows, they can become stuck because of paint buildup that collects on the frame and window joint. To solve this problem, simply cut through the excess paint in the joint.

If a window has been painted shut, you may free it by slipping a thin-bladed knife between the sash and frame to break the paint seal.

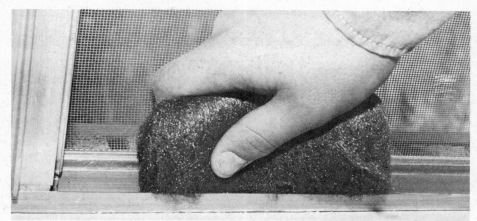

If a slide-by window becomes stuck or sticky, clean dirt from the track, polish the track with steel wool, and lubricate with graphite.

Casement windows may become inoperable because the crank mechanism needs lubrication. Check sill for dirt jamming the window.

Humidity and other weather conditions may interfere with opening of windows. Lubricate casement edges if you cannot adjust it.

REPLACING A BROKEN WINDOW PANE

Many people blanch at the prospect of fixing a broken window, but it really is not a particularly difficult job. The hard part is cutting the new glass exactly to fit the window. It is best that you have your glass dealer do this for you; the service is included in the price of the glass, and he or she can do it quickly and accurately from the measurements you provide.

STEP 1: REMOVING THE BROKEN GLASS

Use heavy gloves and wear goggles or sunglasses to protect your eyes. Grip a broken section of the glass and rock it back and forth until it comes free. If the glass is still held tightly in place, tap the pieces out with a hammer.

STEP 2: SCRAPING OUT OLD PUTTY AND REMOVING POINTS

Use a chisel or putty knife to remove all the old putty from the window. Scrape down to the bare wood. Brush away all loose material.

As you remove the glass, you will see little metal devices in the frame; these are glazier's points. These devices hold the glass in place, not the putty. Pull each of these out with a pair of pliers.

STEP 3: MEASURING AND ORDERING THE GLASS

Next, measure the inside of the frame, both length and width, at least twice. Make sure you get the same figures twice in a row so you can be confident that the measurements are accurate.

When you go to the glass dealer to order the glass, bring your tape measure with you. Surprisingly, tape measures differ in actual size and the glazier's tape or rule might differ from yours. This could result in his cutting a piece that is too small or too large. When you order the glass, you should specify if it is to be single- or double-strength. Ask for double-strength for large windows. If you are not sure, ask the dealer for advice.

Give the dealer your dimensions. He

Clean out all residue of glass and putty and pull all old glazier's points. Scrape the sash as clean as possible. Wear gloves to protect your hands from any fragments of glass.

Measure the inside of the window frame carefully. Check and recheck the measurements and write them down. This will save you from a possible mistake and assure the proper size glass.

The glass is held in place by glazier's points. The points are pushed into the sash frame. Tabs determine how deep they go into the wood. Small projecting ears hold glass in place.

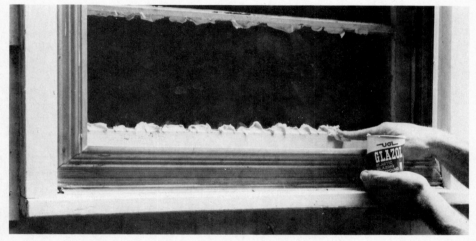

Glazing compound is spread around the edge of the sash. This hides the glazier's points, seals the edges from air and water leaks and prevents the glass from rattling in the wind.

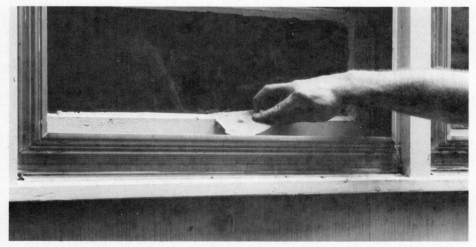

Use a putty knife to trim off the excess glazing compound and to create a smooth and even finish to the surface. Glazing compound does not dry out and will remain securely in place.

(or she) will cut a piece of glass that is fractionally smaller than the size you give him. This will allow for the expansion and contraction of the window frame so that it will not apply undue pressure on the glass.

Buy a small can of glazing compound (not putty) and a box of glazier's points. Get points with small metal projections that allow pressure to be applied for installation.

STEP 4: INSTALLING THE GLASS
Preparing the Frame
Before installing the glass, coat the window frame with a fresh coat of exterior paint. Next, apply a cardboard-thin coating of compound where the glass will rest; this will insure that the wood will not suck the moisture out of the compound that will seal the window, weakening the installation.

Setting the Glass
Insert the glass, pressing it in place gently but solidly. Push the glazier's points into the frame with a putty knife or screw driver. The projecting metal parts will let you do this easily.

Finally, apply the glazing compound. This is superior to putty because it stays soft and flexible indefinitely. Use a putty knife to apply the glazing compound to one side at a time. Dab on small amounts of compound, then run the flat side of the putty knife along the glass and wood to trim it off.

Shape the joint to look like the compound on adjacent windows. Let the compound set for a day, then give it a coat of exterior paint.

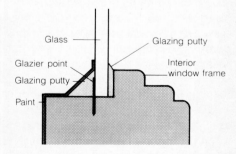

Repaint the frame to finish the job. The film of paint will seal the edges between the glazing compound, the glass and the sash frame.

10

Finishing and Decorating Wood

Now that you have stripped your woodwork, windows, doors, railings, bannisters, paneling, or built-ins, you can make a decision on the refinishing. There are several points to consider before making your choices.

STYLE QUESTIONNAIRE
What Is The Style Of Your Home?
In Colonial times, homeowners used paint as the finish for the woodwork. The paint was often a color other than white. The woodwork might be painted a rich blue, a warm red, a dark green or a gold.

Victorian homes usually had stained and shellacked woodwork. However, when it was economically impossible to use the fine woods that would look best with a clear finish, home builders created imitation wood grain or marble (faux marbre) on inexpensive wood.

Tudor style homes were done with fine, carved wood interior paneling and heavy, exposed wood beams.

Eighteenth century styles were decorated with paint and gilt highlights, as well as murals on the walls.

In contrast, contemporary homes usually employ either natural wood finishes or painted finishes—and even plastic finishes—in the interior woodwork and paneling.

What Style Is Your Furniture?
Your room and your furniture should be compatible, even if they are not entirely in the same style. Because people move more frequently now than they did generations ago, furniture purchased for one home may have to be used in several different homes. Try to minimize the extreme differences between period fur-

The owner of this home chose to combine painted woodwork and cabinets and clear finish. The attention focuses on the fireplace.

Certain architectural styles are best finished with paint. Colonial and early American architectural details are usually painted.

niture and a contemporary home or contemporary furniture and a period home.

What Impression Do You Want your Room to Make?
Ask yourself: Do you want your rooms to appear formal or casual? Do you like the mood created by cool colors or by warm colors? Is the house the focus of attention? Are activities the center of family life?

How Is the Room to Be Used?
If the room you will be refinishing is a formal, lightly used area, your choices

can be made on the basis of appearance only. However, if you are working on a room that will be a center of family activity, especially for smaller children, your main consideration will probably be durability and ease of maintenance.

What Is Your Personal Preference?
You will have to live in the room when it is finished. Although the style of your home may seem to dictate certain choices, you can break some of the "rules" to suit your own taste. For example, choose paint instead of clear finish or clear finish instead of paint on woodwork, de-

Clear finishes were used in this room on a parquet forehearth, mantel and ceiling molding to contrast with a painted window frame and walls.

The woodwork in this room was painted to make it less conspicuous. Attention is given to the super graphic design on the wall.

This child's room is bright and cheerful, a combination of light colors, white paneling and drapery reflect the generous window light.

pending on your preference. On the other hand, it is not advisable to combine too many elements. This is one good rule of thumb despite individual taste.

If you are not sure of what you want or what would be suitable for the style of your house, do a little research. Ask your librarian for suggestions of books to look at. You can also study room photographs that appear in magazines.

How Attractive Is the Wood?

If you have painstakingly stripped the paint from your woodwork and have discovered moldings and millwork of fine maple, or even mahogany, you will undoubtedly want to use some kind of clear finish. If, however, you have stripped the paint away and found Clear pine, you are faced choosing between having uninteresting woodwork or just painting it again. You also can consider giving this wood a specialty finish (these alternatives are discussed in depth in Chapter 11).

Another possibility is to stain the plain wood in a warm color and give it a final,

Contrasting paint colors draw attention to the slanting ceiling line and the unusual style window. The lighter color makes the relatively low ceiling seem to be a little higher.

clear finish to enrich the appearance. Because of the wide range of colors available in stain these days, it is quite possible to change the appearance of pine so that it more closely resembles another wood.

USING STAINS, CLEAR FINISHES AND FILLERS

Before making a choice, determine the balance and harmony you wish to attain in the room. Choose a stain that will be appropriate to the color of your floor (assuming that the room is not fully carpeted) and that will complement the wood in your furniture.

WORKING WITH STAIN
Step 1: Testing the Color
Test the color before you apply it to your woodwork. If possible, use a piece of scrap wood of the same type as the woodwork in your room. If you cannot do this, then do your testing on wood that will not be obvious. The inside of a closet door is one good place. Base molding that is usually hidden by a sofa or another large piece of furniture is another. Apply the stain, wipe off some at varying intervals, and choose the look you like best.

Step 2: Preparing the Surface
If you are working in a confined space or if the molding is attached to a wall you do not want stained, mask off the wall with newspaper and masking tape. Because the stain will soak through the newspaper quickly, place a layer of plastic wrap or aluminum foil on the wall before taping down the paper.

Step 3: Applying the Stain
Apply the stain with a piece of folded

It is easier to test stain on a piece of scrap molding. Apply stain, let set and wipe off; check time to determine how long to leave the stain on the wood to achieve the color wanted.

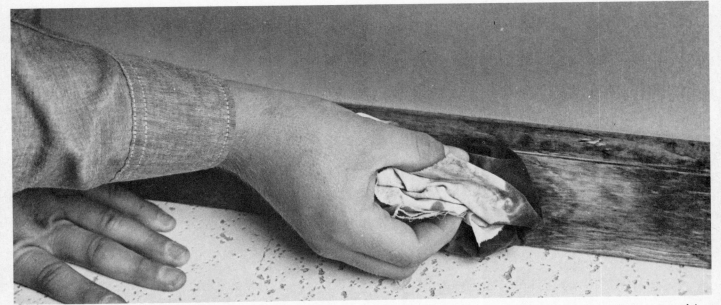

While it may be easier to apply stain to molding that has been removed from the wall, any wood may be stained in place, if you are careful.

Project continued on next page

Stain may be applied with a brush for a rapid, even application. However, extra care must be taken to prevent the stain from dripping or running onto the floor or other surfaces.

cloth or a brush. If you are working on narrow strips of molding, such as a chair rail, a brush is the better choice. Apply the stain in long smooth strokes and allow it to stand long enough to reach the color density you desire. Wipe off the excess stain with a clean cloth.

WORKING WITH FILLER
If the wood in your home is oak, or another open-pore wood, you will probably find your finish application more attractive if you fill the wood with a filler.

As you did with the furniture and the floor, choose a filler that matches or can be dyed to match the stain you

have chosen. Apply across the grain, allow to set a few minutes, and then rub firmly all along the grain to force the filler into the wood. Clean off any excess on the surface before applying the final finish.

There will be directions provided with the filler. Observe the directions and follow them carefully. Filler will make the surface smooth, but if not properly applied—that is, if you do not fill the pores well or allow the filler to dry on the surface—the finish will not look good. Sand and seal the stained and filled surface.

APPLYING CLEAR FINISHES
The technique for applying clear fin-

ishes to woodwork are the same as for applying these finishes to furniture. Reread Chapter 5 and purchase a piece of molding on which to practice application techniques so you can get the feeling of working on a vertical surface.

Using Shellac
Many older homes were finished with shellacked woodwork. The advantages are the same as those given earlier for floors and furniture. Shellac is relatively easy to apply and dries quickly. You can apply as many as three coats of shellac to molding in a room in one day.

However, shellac is not appropriate in any room with high humidity or heavy water use, because the finish will cloud and waterspot.

Using Varnish
Either a polyurethane or regular varnish will give a fine finish, either high gloss or satin, to wood in the home. You will, of course, have to observe precautions of protecting the surfaces from dust and fingerprints. Even "quick-drying" varnish needs twenty-four hours to dry between coats. You will find that the refinishing process takes time.

The advantages of varnish are obvious, however, because of the durability of the finish. You also have a choice of appearances. In an older or Victorian home, the high-gloss varnish will provide an appropriate look.

Using an Oil Finish
Because the oil penetrates the surface, it gives remarkable protection against moisture. However, the application takes time and requires rubbing to achieve the kind of rich glow usually desired in an oil finish.

If you have expanses of built-in furniture and natural wood paneling, you may find nothing else that approaches the quality and beauty of an oil finish. A dining room with a built-in buffet, china closet and paneling is the ideal place for application of an oil finish. You will be required to add repeated coats over a period of months, but the end result will be rewarding.

Stain and sealer may be applied quickly to large expanses, such as paneling, with a soft cloth. Use a drop cloth to protect the floor.

Final, clear finishes are applied with a brush. Load the brush with enough varnish or shellac to flow on freely but not enough to drip.

USING PAINT FINISHES

Enamel is the usual alternative to stain and clear finish on millwork. White and cream are the two most popular colors, but your room style and general decor may make other colors more appropriate to your home.

CHOOSING PAINT
Surface Finishes

Enamel, either latex or oil-base, is available in both a high-gloss and a semi-gloss. The high-gloss paint can give a glassy finish when it is applied properly. High-gloss enamel is sometimes used in kitchens and baths because of the appearance and the ease of maintenance. However, it is more difficult to apply because any brushmarks are so obvious; the highly reflective surface scatters the light and all the irregularities show. This means that the wood surface must be very smooth and the paint must be applied in several thin coats and the coats sanded between applications.

The semi-gloss dries to a soft, smooth finish. It is also likely to show brushmarks, but the marks are less apparent because of the difference in the quality of reflectivity. For the smoothest application, you should sand between coats of this paint.

Latex or Oil-based Paint Choices

Latex Paint There is a definite appeal to most do-it-yourselfers in latex paint. It is easy to mix; it is thick so that it clings to a brush without spattering easily; the brushes can be washed with soap and water. The paint also dries very quickly. Even an enamel latex paint will dry to the touch in an hour. There is a strong odor to the paint, but the fumes are less ob-

Large, immovable objects, such as heating units, may be made less conspicuous by painting to match a surrounding area.

A semi-gloss or flat enamel is the best choice for surfaces that have to be washed often, such as the walls and furniture in a child's room.

Project continued on next page

Dip a brush no more than one-third to one-half the length of the bristles. Paint is applied with the ends of the bristles.

Stroke the brush smoothly and let the paint flow off the brush onto the surface. Paint wet into wet and plan logical stopping points.

noxious and certainly less toxic than oil-based paint.

However, there is a question of durability. Latex paint washes well, but if washed too soon after application—as may be required in a child's room or a bath—the paint may wear away more quickly than expected. Occasionally, a latex paint will waterspot or stain. You would be well advised to test the paint you are considering if you plan to use it in a bathroom.

Oil-based Paint The standard formulation until some twenty years ago, oil-base paint is slightly more difficult to use than latex and considerably more difficult to clean up. A thinner material, oil-base paint requires careful attention during application. A painter is more likely to spatter an adjacent wall when applying this paint than when using latex.

The durability of oil-base paint is very high. Back entry areas or basement stairs in some older homes may still be wearing coats of paint applied thirty or forty years ago. The paint may be a dull gray color, but the finish has survived the constant abuse.

Because of the thinners and vehicle used to carry the pigment in this paint, there is a recognizable and sometimes objectionable odor to oil-base paint. Most homeowners prefer to use oil-base paints during warm weather so that they can leave the windows open to keep air moving through the areas being painted.

Cleanup of brushes requires the use of paint thinner, turpentine or a special brush cleaner. Because this is time-consuming and bothersome, many people choose to wait until the entire project is finished before cleaning their brushes. To do this, wrap your brush in plastic wrap and then in aluminum foil. Store the brush in your refrigerator overnight or in the freezer for a longer period. This will keep the paint from drying.

APPLYING THE PAINT

You may use either a natural bristle or nylon bristle brush for oil-base paint. Use only a nylon or other synthetic bristle brush for latex paint.

If you have any doubts about your skill in applying paint, mask any adjacent areas you do not wish to paint. Use newspaper and masking tape. Use drop clothes on the floor and cover or remove all furniture in the room. This will save many hours of repairing "mistakes" that you may make as you work.

Brush the paint in long, steady strokes. Whenever possible, make a continuous stroke from top to bottom or from end to end of a section. This

Mask off adjoining walls when painting wood-work. This will mean less cleanup and repair when you have finished the painting project.

Latex paint will wash out of a brush with soap and water. Clean a brush until bristles are clean and rinse water runs clean. Paint trapped in the brush will dry and make it useless.

is nearly impossible if you are painting base molding or chair rails. Try to reach from one joint to the next in a smooth stroke. If you cannot do this, work as quickly as you can to apply the paint, then stroke the brush over the entire section in one smooth movement to even the surface.

In most rooms, application to the woodwork of smooth coats of plain enamel produces an attractive, finished look.

CLEANUP
Repairing Mistakes

Even the most careful painter will have some drips or accidents. Provide yourself with plenty of rags so that an emergency can be handled immediately. If you act fast enough, most paint can be entirely wiped up without difficulty. If you spill paint on carpeting, you can soak up and soak out latex

paint. Immediate action with rags will soak up most oil-base paint. But you will have to use solvent cleaner to remove the residue from the carpeting. The cleaner may cause as much damage as the paint. If you spatter paint, wipe it up immediately. Quick action is the best. Spatters on varnish floors or tile or vinyl flooring may be scraped off carefully. Use a single-edge razor blade to gently scrape the spatters off.

Cleaning your Brushes

Latex paint will come out of brushes with water rinsing and soap and water washing. Hang the brush, bristles down, to dry.

Oil-base paint will come out of brushes with a solvent. The easiest way to remove the paint is to insert a dowel through the hole in the brush handle and to suspend the brush in a can or jar of paint thinner. The paint

eventually will settle to the bottom.

After the brush has soaked for several hours, wipe off as much of the paint and thinner as possible. Wash the brush with strong detergent and water.

Pour off the clean, top section of the paint thinner or brush cleaner and save it for reuse. Dispose of the residue in a safe and ecologically acceptable manner. Check with your local governmental office (such as city hall) for guidance as to safe dumping procedures for your area. The types of questions to ask include:

(1) Can you flush it away?
(2) Can you put it into the garbage?
(3) Do you have to take it to a pre-determined dumping site?

11

Specialized Finishes for Woodwork

Just as it is possible to use a variety of special finishes on furniture, the same finishes can be used on doors, windows, woodwork and even picture frames. The materials and techniques are the same as those used on furniture. The only differences arise in how and where the finishes are applied. Doors and window units can be removed from their frames; it is also possible—although very time consuming and difficult—to pry molding from your walls so it can be refinished on a workbench. In many cases, however, you will have to work on wood that is firmly attached to walls or floors.

PREPARING FOR SPECIAL FINISHING

There are two steps to preparation: practice and protection. The first is obvious. If you make a mistake in application techniques, you will either have to live with the look you achieve or start all over. Woodwork cannot be moved into another room to hide the "bad spots". Practice on scrap wood until you are absolutely secure about each step in the refinishing procedure.

If you are going to be finishing base-molding or chair rails in place on the walls, protect the walls with newspaper and masking tape. No matter how neat a person you are, you can spatter the wall if you have just a little too much paint, stain or glaze on your brush. If your arm trembles as you tire, the brush may slip off the molding onto the wall. Always place drop cloths on your floor.

CHOOSING A SPECIAL FINISH

Your choice of a special finish must be considered carefully. Too much of a good thing may be unbearable. If you

A photo-realist super graphic is an unusual decorative feature in this room. This type of hand-painted finish work is beyond the scope of the average person but other paint work is not.

Carved moldings can be emphasized by the manner in which they are painted. Highlighting or precise trim painting are possible.

Selective painting of raised areas of this molding creates a special pattern and visual focus for this wall covered with square panels.

used a highlighting technique in refinishing a rococco style table and you liked the result, think carefully before highlighting the woodwork in the room in which the table sits. What is attractive in the table may be overwhelming in the woodwork.

The character of the woodwork itself also dictates the suitability of some finishes. Highlighting works on curved and carved wood. If your woodwork consists of flat boards trimmed with quarter-round strips as shoe and top molding, highlighting will not work. On the other hand, trimmed brick molding, which has grooves and a step-back pattern, would be appropriate for highlighting. The flat wood molding is a good candidate for an attractive antiqued, pickled, or grained finish. You might consider these finishes for use on paneling, too.

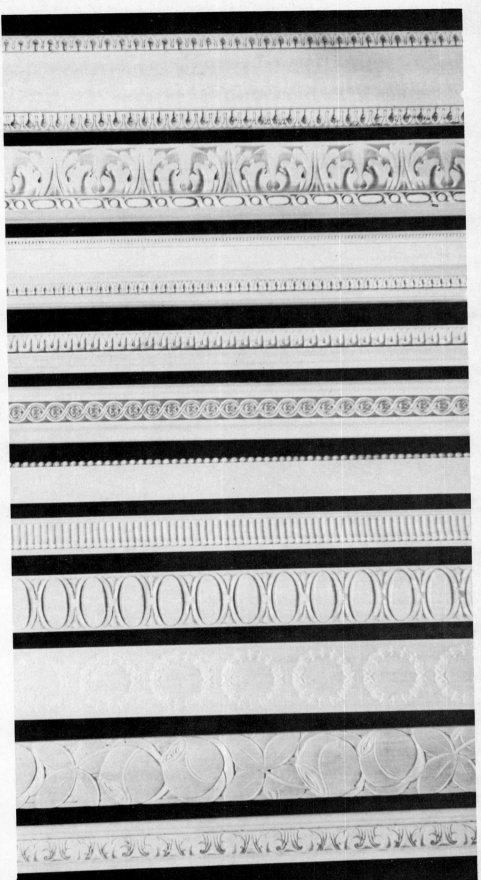

Wood and/or plaster trimmed moldings come in a wide variety of sizes and styles. These may be painted one or more colors or highlighted with metallic or contrasting color.

STENCILING A FLOOR OR WALL

In certain rooms, stenciling will be very attractive and appropriate. Colonial and early American style homes are logical and appropriate places for stenciling on the floors. Because of the cost of importing carpeting was very high before domestic industry was developed, many people painted their floors and patterned them with stenciled designs. Stencil patterns also are appropriate on the walls of homes in a casual or rustic style. The stenciled borders are usually found, however, on walls rather than on woodwork. Pattern borders above chair rails or just below the ceiling molding are two common stencil locations.

APPLICATION OF STENCIL PATTERNS

Application of stencil patterns to walls is exactly like that used for furniture; however, you may experience more problems just maintaining the even spacing and level positioning of the stencils when you are working above eye level.

Step 1: Wall Preparation

Prepare the wall by marking the proper locations with snapped chalklines. Use a spirit level to check alignment of your patterns.

Use a spirit level to determine the horizontal line needed for your stencil pattern and then mark that position with a chalkline.

Step 2: Testing Stencil Pattern and Placement

You may find it advisable to test the look of the stencil positions before painting the stencils. Tape the stencil into place and fill the stencil pattern with chalk dust applied with a pounce bag. If you cannot find a pounce bag, grind a light-colored piece of chalk in a pencil sharpener and wrap the dust in a bag made of several layers of cheesecloth. Apply the chalk dust by bumping the pounce bag over the open areas of the stencil. Remove the stencil mask and you will see a faint pattern. There will be enough of an impression for you to tell whether you have put the stencil on straight and if the spacing is correct. Remove the chalk dust with a soft brush. Any residue can be wiped away with a kneaded rubber eraser.

Step 3: Applying to the Wall

The technique of applying the paint to the wall is exactly like that of applying to furniture. The lacquer-type paint is applied with the same brush technique. The brush should not have a great deal of paint on it. The lacquer dries quickly and is not likely to run or drip. However, protect the wall below and above the stencil mask with newspaper held up with masking tape.

Position your stencil where you think you want the design. Use a pounce bag, filled with chalk dust or other powder, to fill in the design on the wall to test the location and pattern.

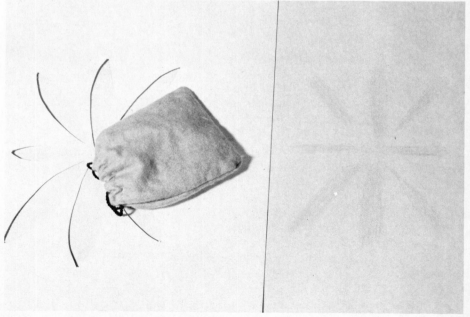

The chalk dust will leave a light but distinctive mark on the wall. Repeat the process until you can see the effect of the stenciling. Blow or gently wipe dust away before painting.

APPLYING SPECIAL FINISHES TO INTERIOR SURFACES

These techniques are discussed in depth in Chapter 6. Please refer to those projects for specific details. The significant difference in applying special finishes to doors, windows, and molding is that the expanses and details are greater than on most pieces of furniture. You will have to plan your work carefully so that you do not create any "seams" in your work.

Graining, antiquing, pickling, highlighting, and mottling all require a base coat. Each of the finishes is applied over a good basecoat; no basecoat should have overlapping, noticeable brushmarks. Neither should there be any overlapping marks in the glazing coat that produces the final finish look.

PRACTICE
Study the wood and decide exactly how you want the finished work to look. If possible, practice on scrap that is set up like the project. Mitre cut two boards and nail them to exposed studs in your garage to simulate a mitre joint in your window or door frame. Practice applying and wiping the glaze until you can achieve the desired effect at will. You will also get practice in wiping out your mistakes. This is a handy and useful skill.

PLAN YOUR WORK
Plan your work in practical sections. Because graining requires particular concentration, plan work in sections small enough to allow yourself regular and frequent breaks. Check the style of your work as you go along. The more confident you become, the more relaxed your work will be. This will show in the finished work. The early sections may have smaller, tighter graining lines; later sections may have broader, freer lines. Trees, of course, do not grow with identical grain patterns, but if you are working your way around a room, the beginning work and the ending work will meet, and the difference may be startling and disconcerting.

It is better to be too conservative than too liberal if you are giving a specialty finish to wood in a large room. Bold and dramatic highlighting, graining or mottling may be so distracting that the room loses all the intended decorative focus. Antiquing and pickling are usually milder in their general effect and may be used to tone down the impression of brightly painted woodwork. Mottling, done wet on dry with similar shades, is also useful for softening the effect of paint that turned out to be brighter than expected.

A light glaze applied over a dark finish, pickling, may give the effect of grain. It will lighten the look of very dark wood or paint.

A graining comb, shown here, will cut into a wet glaze coat to reveal part of the basecoated surface. It can be used to create an interesting pattern or a simulated wood grain.

A mottled finish can be applied with crumpled paper, an uneven brush or rough cloth. Apply wrinkled paper to a smooth glaze coat and a mottled pattern appears when the paper is removed.

SPECIALTY FINISHES ON PICTURE FRAMES

In general, picture frames are made of wood molding. If you have a frame you wish to refinish, handle it exactly like any other wood in stripping and refinishing.

Be careful in handling the frame. The corners are mitered and held by fine brads and glue. If you use a large quantity of stripper, you may weaken the glue. The brads are too light to hold the sections together without the glue.

REPAIRING WOOD MOLDING FRAMES

Regluing Mitre Joints

If the joints have become weak, you can pull the frame apart and remake the joints. Use a tack hammer to tap out the brads. Scrape away the glue residue and sand the mitre cut edges very lightly to remove the last of the glue.

Tap new brads into the holes that exist in the corner of one of the pieces. Apply white glue to the edges of the mitre joint and press the pieces together. Hold the joint square and tap the brads all the way into the second piece at the corner, countersinking with a fine nail. The brads hold the frame until the glue dries. Repeat with the other two pieces for the other corner. When both sections are dry and secure, put the two sections together to remake the whole frame.

Repairs for Gouges and Mars

If you are going to give the frame an antique finish, you need not repair any gouges or nicks. If you want a smooth and even finish, however, you will have to fill these just as you filled the gouges in furniture and moldings, using a wood putty or lacquer stick.

REFINISHING PICTURE FRAMES

If the molding is attractive and a natural finish is appropriate to the drawing, painting or photo that you will put in the frame, you can stain the wood and give the frame a clear finish.

Many frames are antiqued or highlighted. In some cases, you may find frame material that is given a base coat, highlighted and then is antiqued. As long as the finish given the frame is appropriate for the item framed, you can use virtually any color and finishing technique combination.

Gilt Frames

Many frames come either all or partly finished in a gilt finish. This is a paint made of fine flakes of metal, usually a bronze powder, suspended in a liquid vehicle and a bonding agent, glue.

As time passes, the metal flakes may wear away or discolor. To restore the finish, clean the surface and apply a new coating of the gilt. Apply with

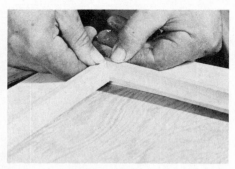

Picture frames are usually constructed of mitre cut wood molding. The corners are glued and held with small wire brads.

a "dry" brush. Because the liquid is thin and the metal flakes move about in the liquid, there is a tendency to use too much at one time. The liquid and suspended flakes then tend to run or puddle, giving the finish a very uneven look. You may have to apply several coats of the thin liquid to give a completely new finish to the frame. Wait several hours or overnight between coats. However, for a fresh look try a light coating with a brush that has been wiped nearly dry.

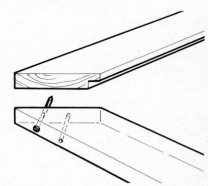

The brads that secure the corners until the glue has dried are driven through very small holes that are predrilled to prevent cracking.

Fine, decorative picture moldings should enhance the artwork they contain and be appropriate to the room in which they are hung. The frame also sets the art off from the wall.

REPAIRING PLASTER COATED PICTURE FRAMES

If you own a 19th century painting or a studio photographic portrait of your great-grandfather, you may also possess an ornate plaster picture frame. These creations are a combination of a wood frame and molded plaster of Paris painted with gilt, or even covered with gold leaf.

These frames are heavy. The more ornate the plaster work, the larger the pieces of wood in the frame must be. Some frames, four feet square and larger, have 2x stock rather than molding as the base of the frame.

Damage commonly occurs when the frame is dropped during moving or when it falls off a wall because the weight of the frame pulls the hanger out of the plaster. If the frame does not shatter when it falls, it will crack at the very least.

REPAIRING CRACKED PLASTER

A crack in a plaster frame is repaired very much like a crack in a plaster wall.

First, determine that there is only a crack rather than a break. If a section of the plaster is loose, you should glue the section to the frame (see below) before attempting to repair the crack. If the section has not pulled completely free of the wood frame, use a piece of thin cardboard, like a playing card or index card, to apply glue to the frame and plaster section. Press the plaster against the frame. This must be done with some care so you do not damage the plaster further. Pad the plaster surface with cotton or soft cloths and tie the section down with heavy, soft yarn.

Re-adhering a Section

If an entire section has broken off, wipe the frame and the back of the piece until it is as free of dust, cracked plaster and glue as possible. Apply fresh glue to the frame. Replace the broken section. Hold with yarn and pads as described above.

Use spackling compound to fill any cracks. Apply it carefully with a toothpick or orangestick. Clean off any excess compound before it sets. If there is a texture in the plaster, try to match it with the compound.

Once the compound has dried, use a fine, sharp knife to cut away any excess. Apply gilt paint to cover the patch and to match the finish. If you have a frame that was originally covered in gold leaf, seek professional advice in making repairs, or simply put the repair in the hands of a professional. Gold leaf is exactly what its name implies—gold that has been beaten into a thin sheet. It is applied to a surface by hand rubbing with a special tool. The process is an acquired skill. Gold leaf is also extremely expensive and is not a material to experiment with.

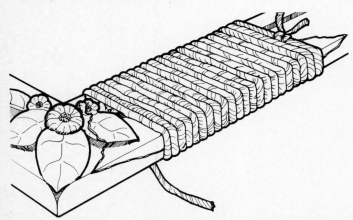

A combination of wood and plaster, this one-hundred-year-old frame is extremely heavy and must be held by a 16d nail driven into a stud.

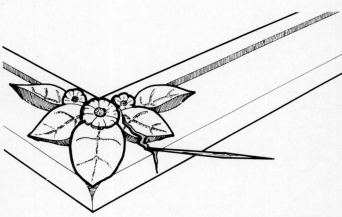

Fill a small crack in a plaster frame with plaster of Paris or other patching compound. Apply with a toothpick or sharpened dowel.

If a large piece cracks off the plaster frame, use white glue to readhere it. Wrap the area with yarn to hold the section in place.

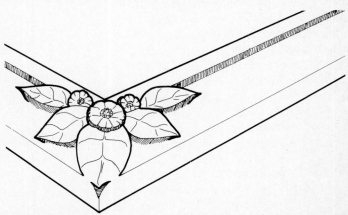

Patched, reglued and repainted with appropriate metallic glaze, this frame should not show any of the marks of breakage or repair.

12
Cleaning Furniture and Other Wood

Now that we have discussed at great length how to strip and refinish wood, we should mention that all wood finishes need care and maintenance. Furthermore, before you consider refinishing any piece of furniture you should discover whether the piece really needs refinishing or is even worth the effort. In some cases, what appears to be a bad finish may be the effect of a buildup of dirt, waxes and oils and minor surface blemishes. In other cases you may be dealing with an antique.

Consider your reaction to the furniture. If you are thinking of refinishing a piece because you have gotten tired of it and are hoping you will like it better, get rid of it. Refinishing is messy and time consuming; you will probably resent the effort involved. However, cleaning a piece of furniture or woodwork may make the wood look so new and attractive that you will not realize it is the same. The effort involved is less, and the results can be spectacular.

CONSIDERATIONS FOR ANTIQUES
If the piece of furniture is an antique, its value will be diminished significantly if you strip and refinish the wood. If you have any questions about the age or value of your furniture, seek the opinion and guidance of an expert or do the research yourself. You will probably be able to get assistance in dating an object from your local library or historical society.

Refinishing or restoration of antiques should be left to qualified professionals. To find professional help, contact a museum in your area that has a collection of antique furniture. They will employ a conservator or will know where you can find one. The conservator is a highly skilled artisan who uses specialized techniques and appropriate materials to retain and reveal original workmanship in antiques, paintings, tapestry, and other art forms. Each area is very specialized; you will be looking for a wood furniture specialist.

Wood furniture is durable and will withstand long-term, heavy use. However, wood finishes are vulnerable to wear and accident. Regular maintenance, cleaning and polishing are needed.

Wood used in kitchens will develop a film of grease that will attract and hold dirt. Clean these wood surfaces often to prevent damage.

Carved wood, such as this mantel, is very attractive, but it will hold soot and other dirt and must be carefully cleaned.

HOW TO RECONDITION WOOD

If the surface of a lacquer or shellac finish has cracked and looks like alligator skin, you can reamalgamate it. If the finish is still smooth, you may be able just to clean and condition the wood. There are many wood cleaners and conditioners on the market, or you can create a homemade conditioner. It will clean the wood, restore the finish, inhibit checking, and remove cloudiness or dullness. At the same time, the conditioner will remove excessive layers of wax that have built up over the years.

STEP 1: MIXING THE CONDITIONER

Make the conditioner from one-quarter cup of gum turpentine (not steam distilled) and three-quarters cup boiled linseed oil. Mix the liquids in a clean glass jar. Cover the jar tightly when not in use; it will store indefinitely.

Use a quart-size glass jar to hold the turpentine/linseed oil conditioner. Keep it tightly covered for safe storage.

Before beginning, you should determine what the finish is. If shellac, use the conditioner sparingly; because of the chemistry involved, the turpentine/oil mixture can cut into the shellac fairly easily. As suggested earlier, apply denatured alcohol to an area of finish that is not easily seen. If the alcohol softens the surface, the finish is shellac.

STEP 2: USING THE CONDITIONER

Work in a well-ventilated area. Place many thicknesses of newspaper on the floor to protect the surrounding areas.

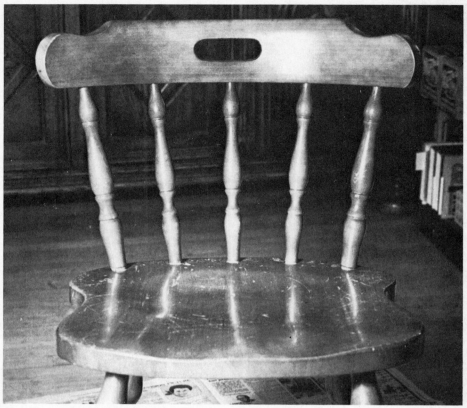

This kitchen chair has received heavy use and has had various liquids and food spilled on it. The chair and basic finish are in good condition, but the finish needs a good cleaning.

Place furniture on newspaper and set the jar, filled with warm water and a thin film of the conditioner, in a plate or pan. Any drips or spills, in a large amount, would soften the finish.

Preparing the Mixture

Heat a pint of water; pour it into a larger container and place the container in a pie plate or saucer to catch any liquid that runs down the side of the container.

Applying the Mixture

Shake the turpentine/oil mixture thoroughly, and pour a thin stream of it into the water; pour just enough to create a film of the oil material on the water. Fold up a clean cloth and dip it into the mixture. Rub a small area of the wood at one time. Use the mixture sparingly on joints because an excess of the conditioner will soften the glue. Use an old toothbrush to get

The conditioner should clean away any surface dirt and lift off most dirt that has worked into the surface of the finish. Follow the application of the conditioner with a good polish.

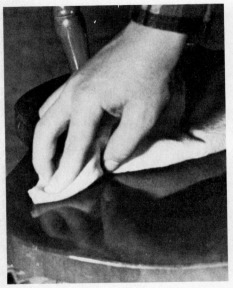

Apply the condition with a soft, clean cloth. Change the cloth when it becomes soiled so you do not rub the dirt back into the finish.

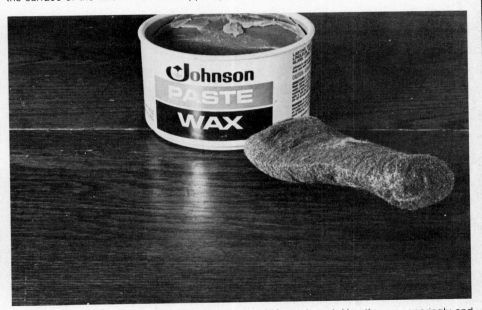

Apply paste wax to a cleaned finish with a pad of 000 steel wool. Use the wax sparingly and work in small sections, applying and polishing as you work. Buff with a soft cloth.

the conditioner into any grooves or turnings.

The soil should lift off as you rub. If it does not, rub with grade 000 steel wool. Always follow the grain as you rub the mixture into the wood.

Removing the Conditioner

When it looks as if the soil is loose, wipe the conditioner and soil away with a warm wet cloth. If the surface is shellac, first wring the rag "dry". Finally, wipe the cleaned area with a clean, dry cloth.

As you work, the mixture will become cold. Discard it—do not try to reheat it. Produce a fresh mixture.

STEP 3: POLISHING THE SURFACE

Despite the conditioning process, some pieces of wood may still seem lifeless or dry. Here, it is recommended that you apply a greaseless furniture cream containing beeswax or apply a paste wax with 000 steel wool.

Applying A Paste Wax

If you use a paste wax and steel wool, use the wax sparingly, and work on only a small area at a time. That is, dab a little wax on a rolled-up piece of the steel wool. Then rub it over a six-inch-square area until the wood takes on the sheen you wish. Turn the steel wool to expose fresh areas as

needed. Repeat the procedure for the rest of the surface. The most common mistake people make with paste wax is to use too much. This leads to creating a gummy surface that attracts dirt and cannot be polished properly.

If the furniture is not dried out, an emulsified cream polish, a lemon-oil polish or a thin oil may be used. If the furniture has a high lustre, use a polish that gives a high gloss, such as Pledge.

ALTERNATIVE 1: REAMALGAMATING THE FINISH

If the surface of your wood is checked, the top layer of finish has dried and cracked. Lacquer and shellac can be reamalgamated. To do this, apply the solvent suitable for the finish (lacquer thinner for lacquer and denatured alcohol for shellac) with a brush or a pad of 000 steel wool. Cover the surface liberally with the solvent. Then rub the surface along the grain of the wood. Work quickly; the solvent evaporates fast. The solvent will dissolve the cracked surface. As you rub the surface to smooth it, the solvent evaporates leaving a smooth surface.

The shellac finish on this clock is badly alligatored because it sat in direct sunlight. Heat and light dried the shellac and it crackled.

Denatured alcohol was applied with a pad of soft cloth. The shellac surface melted into the solvent and the dried to a smooth finish.

ALTERNATIVE 2: POLISHING WITH ROTTENSTONE AND OIL

If the surface has taken on a dull and worn look because of many, very small scratches, or the surface of varnish is lightly alligatored, you may restore the finish by polishing with rottenstone and oil. Pour rottenstone into a small dish or saucer and mix with light oil. Dip a soft cloth or felt pad into the paste mixture and rub on the finish in the direction of the grain.

Rub until the surface feels smooth. Wipe the rottenstone paste off with another soft cloth. Examine the surface; if it seems to have reached the luster you want, apply the paste to another area and polish. If you want a higher luster, reapply paste and rub more. When you have finished, clean the surface with lemon oil or wood furniture cleaner. Then polish with a wax or other polish appropriate to the surface finish.

Rottenstone and oil were mixed on the lightly alligatored varnish surface of this old oak dining table. The mix was rubbed with cheesecloth.

The cheesecloth picked up most of the rottenstone and oil mixture. The mixture was rubbed with the grain with gentle pressure.

The rubbing wore away the alligatored varnish and polished the surface smooth. Shallow scratches in the varnish were also removed.

CLEANING AND POLISHING YOUR FURNITURE

It is a good idea to polish furniture regularly. In doing this, you should become acquainted with types of furniture care products available, and read the labels to find out which products will do an effective cleaning job on your furniture. Follow specific instructions for use given by manufacturers of the products in order to obtain best results. No single product is effective for all finishes. Note that too frequent use of polishes and waxes will build up the material on the surface and reduce the beauty of the finish.

PRODUCING A HOMEMADE POLISH

Mix equal parts of: denatured alcohol, strained, fresh lemon juice (not canned or frozen), olive oil, and gum turpentine (not synthetic or steam-distilled). To use, shake well, and apply with a clean, absorbent, lintless cloth. Follow by rubbing the piece with a dry cloth, removing all excess. Finally, polish with a dry woolen cloth.

CLEANING LEATHER AND VINYL

Although most pieces of furniture are mostly wood, some may be partly leather or plastic. In some older homes, you may even find some leather insets in wood paneling. These items also require cleaning.

Using Leather Cleaner

To clean leather, dampen a sponge in warm water and wring dry. Rub over a bar of castile soap or in a can of saddle soap. Squeeze the sponge to work up a good lather. Rub the leather briskly. Use a clean, soft cloth to wipe the soap off the leather; then rub briskly with a soft, dry cloth to restore sheen.

Using a Leather Dressing

If the leather appears dried, rub a small amount of leather dressing into the leather to replace oil. You can buy a leather dressing or make one, using ingredients available at saddle shops and drugstores and listed below.

60% pure neat's foot oil, a by-product of cattle bones

40% anhydrous lanolin, a natural oil found in wool.

To mix: Place lanolin in a container large enough to hold all the lanolin and the neat's foot oil. Warm the container of lanolin in hot water until it has melted. Slowly add neat's foot oil, stirring until blended. When the mixture has cooled, apply a small amount of the dressing to the leather with your fingertips. Rub until the dressing is completely absorbed. Rub tooled areas gently. Close the jar tightly. This dressing stores indefinitely.

Leather upholstery must be cleaned and conditioned regularly or it will become dry and brittle. The seat of this eighty-five year old chair has had neat's foot oil worked into it.

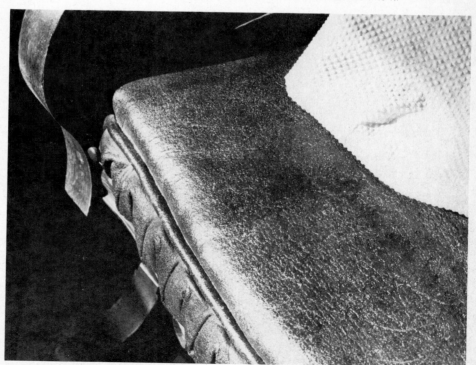

The leather surface is rubbed and polished. Small scratches in the leather fade as the conditioner softens the leather. The leather takes on an attractive luster as it is polished.

CLEANING LAMINATED PLASTIC

To clean plastic, dip a cloth into the light suds of a hand dishwashing liquid and warm water; squeeze and wipe the surface. Dip another cloth into clear, warm water; squeeze, wipe the surface, and then dry. If slight staining occurs on solid colors, dust whiting or baking soda on the stain to absorb and bleach the stain out. Wipe gently with a damp cloth or sponge. Dry.

CLEANING VINYL UPHOLSTERY

Your best choice is to clean the vinyl as directed by the manufacturer. If you have lost these directions, sponge the vinyl with warm water and mild dishwashing liquid. Leave the soapy water on the surface a few minutes to loosen soil. Rub briskly, repeat, rinse, and dry.

Remove grease and oily spots with vinyl cleaner (available in departments or stores that stock vinyl upholstery), warm water, and a sponge. Once or twice yearly, sponge with a mixture of vinyl cleaner and warm water. Brush the surface with a soft, wet brush, rinse and wipe dry.

To remove stains, first moisten a cloth in equal parts of denatured alcohol solvent and water or full-strength rubbing alcohol. Next apply saddle soap; wipe with a damp cloth and then with a dry cloth.

Vinyl upholstery, especially on kitchen chairs, often receives hard use and is touched by soiled hands. To clean the upholstery, use a vinyl cleaner or a mild detergent and a soft sponge.

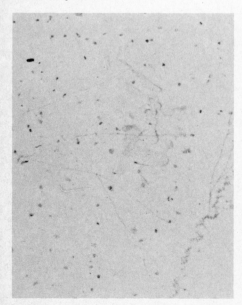

Plastic laminate is a popular counter surface because it is easy to clean and durable. Laminate is vulnerable to stains and scratches.

Wet the area of a stain and apply a heavy coating of baking soda. Some of the stain will soak into the baking soda.

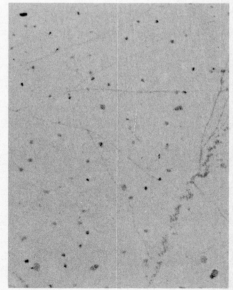

Rub the remaining baking soda with a wet cloth. The soda is a mild abrasive and will scrub off most remaining stains and dirt.

CLEANING PANELING

If you have natural wood paneling in your home, as opposed to the prefinished type that has a plastic coating and does not lend itself to refinishing, you will be able to use the same cleaning methods discussed for any wood. There are special products for cleaning and polishing natural wood paneling; you may use those, too.

If you have plastic finished paneling, it can be cleaned with warm water, pieces of towel and a strong detergent. Mix the detergent as directed. Observe three things: keep your wiping rags clean, keep the water clean—change it frequently—and always work from the bottom of the wall up. If you wash from the top down the solution may run down the panels and create streaks which are difficult to remove.

Of course, certain areas in paneling may become particularly worn and dirty. Even plastic finishes can become worn. Clean regularly. Make a paste of water and baking soda to create a non-abrasive cleaner for plastic.

Paneling given an oil finish can be renewed quickly with an additional application of the oil finish material after cleaning.

Natural wood paneling may have an oiled or varnished finish. This paneling should be treated in the same way you treat oiled or varnished furniture. Condition and polish regularly.

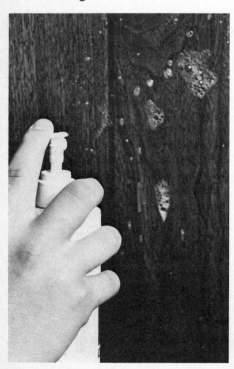

Plastic finished paneling can be spot cleaned with a good spray cleaner. Do this often or the dirt will penetrate the plastic surface.

Plastic finish panels should be washed at regularly, every year or so, to keep it fresh and attractive. Grooved paneling should be dusted weekly to avoid any accumulation of dirt.

Glossary

Abrasive Any material used to wear away, smooth or polish a surface, such as sandpaper used to smooth wood.

Alligatored finish Any finished surface that shows cracks caused by aging and drying.

Anhydrous lanolin A natural oil, from wool, that has had all water removed.

Antiquing A decorative finish process. A basecoat is covered with a glaze, another paint, stain or varnish, that is partly wiped or brushed away to reveal some of the basecoat color.

Banister An upright piece, often turned or carved, that supports a handrail for a stairway.

Breathing mask A device to cover the nose and mouth and prevent inhalation of dust or other material in the air.

Casement window A window that opens on a hinge on one side. A casement window is often controlled by a crank.

Clear finish Any of a number of wood finishes that allow the wood grain to be seen.

Coloring stick A type of colored wax crayon that will hide small scratches in finished wood.

Conservator A craftsman who specializes in cleaning, preserving and restoring works of fine art and antiques.

Danish oil A penetrating oil finish used on Danish modern style furniture.

Decoupage A decorative process in which printed paper illustrations are applied to a surface and coated with many layers of clear varnish.

Denatured alcohol A solvent used to thin shellac.

Distressing A finishing process that adds dents, scratches, burns and other indications of wear and age to furniture for decorative reasons.

Double-hung window A standard window style containing two sections of movable sash, usually a lower section that can be raised and an upper one that can be lowered.

Dowel A wood pin frequently used to join two pieces of wood. The dowel fits into holes drilled in each piece; this creates a dowel joint.

Fad A piece of wadded cotton that is the core of the rubber for a French polish.

Fasteners Nails, screws, brads and other items that are used to join two items or to secure hardware to furniture or millwork.

Faux Marbre Imitation marble created through skillful application of painted marble finish patterns.

Finish flooring Any material such as parquet, tongue and groove planks or continuous floor covering that is laid over subflooring. The exposed flooring.

Flitch A sheet of veneer.

French polish A shellac finish applied in many layers with a rubber. The surface is sanded between coats with fine, oiled sandpaper. The final coat is often polished with rottenstone and oil.

Gilt A metallic finish material in which metal flakes and an adhesive are suspended in a volatile liquid.

Glazier's points Small metal devices that hold a pane of glass in place against the frame. A small point is pushed into the frame to a depth determined by a small flange; two additional flanges hold glass.

Gold leaf A tissue-thin sheet of pure gold that is applied to a surface by direct rubbing.

Grain The growth pattern in the tree. The grain will look different in different trees and as a result of different sawing techniques.

Graining A specialty finish used to create the impression of wood grain with paint. Imitation wood grain.

Graphite powder A ground soft carbon material that is a dry lubricant.

Hardwood Wood that is cut from deciduous (leaf-shedding) trees. Although all such wood is designated as hardwood, some types are actually physically soft and easy to dent.

Highlighting A decorative technique used on some carved or turned wood, usually an application of metallic paint over a basecoat. The metallic paint is wiped off the surface before drying. This leaves a metallic residue in the grooves.

Joists A structural framework of 2x6s or larger stock running from exterior walls to a center girder. These joists are usually 16 inches apart and support the subflooring.

Lac beetle An insect that secretes a fluid which is made into lac flakes, the basic ingredient in shellac.

Lacquer A clear or colored finish material that dries to a hard, glossy finish. Usually applied with a sprayer, lacquer dries too quickly for smooth application with a brush.

Lacquer/shellac sticks Sticks of filler material used in the repair of surface damage to furniture. The filler must be melted onto the damaged surface and then trimmed smooth.

Lally columns Support columns found in basements. These columns support a girder that runs perpendicular to and supports the joists.

Linseed oil A finishing oil made from pressed flax seeds. An ingredient used in paint (oil-base) and varnish.

Millwork Manufactured wood molding, doors and windows.

Molding Various types of wood used for decorative or practical trim. Molding styles range from flat lath to ornately grooved, carved or stamped picture frame moldings. It is usually applied to cover joints of dissimilar surfaces such as basemolding at junctures of walls and floors.

Mortise and tenon A joint in which one piece has a square or rectangular projection that fits snugly into a similarly shaped hole in the second piece.

Mottling A decorative finish. A basecoat of one flat color is largely or lightly covered with another color or material applied in some way to give an uneven finish. For example a white surface may be blotted with a sponge dampened with walnut stain.

Neat's foot oil A fatty oil derived from cattle bones. This product is a conditioner that may be used on leather upholstery.

Oil finish A clear finish produced by rubbing an oil, such as linseed, into bare or stained wood. The oil is rubbed to a soft, glowing finish.

Paint A pigmented varnish (oil-based) material that will completely cover and hide the surface to which it is applied. Newer formulas combine rubber (latex) and water.

Parquet A wood flooring material made into blocks or tiles. A finish wood flooring in a decorative design.

Pick stick A combination of varnish and rosin and cotton designed to pick dust and lint from a damp varnish surface.

Pickling A wood finish originally created by bleaching the wood surface with caustic chemicals. Imitiated today by wiping a light-color glaze on and off a darker basecoat.

Plain sawing Cutting a log straight along the length creating boards with various grain patterns. This sawing creates a certain amount of waste but allows for cutting the widest possible boards from the tree.

Polyurethane A varnish to which plastics have been added. It creates a durable finish.

Pounce bag A cloth bag containing chalk dust or other powder that leaves a dust mark on any surface on which the bag is hit

Pumice A lava rock abrasive, pumice is ground into a powder for a polish.

Quarter sawing A method of sawing boards from quarter sections of a log. The process creates some very narrow boards that are waste. The resulting grain pattern is more attractive and the cut boards stronger than those created by plain sawing.

Raising the grain A process of damping the surface of wood to bring up or lift small fibers for final smooth sanding.

Rasp A rough sided tool designed to dig into and wear away material such as wood.

Reamalgamated finish A previously alligatored or roughened finish that has been made level by rubbing the surface with solvent that melts the finish and lets it dry smooth.

Respirator A filter device worn over the nose and mouth to remove irritants—dust and toxic matter—from the air before it is inhaled.

Rosemaling A folk painting style often used on furniture, ceilings and interior moldings in Norwegian homes.

Rotary sawing A sawing technique in which a blade inserted into a rotating log peels a continuous thin layer to create a veneer flitch or a plywood ply.

Riff sawing A technique similar to quarter sawing in which narrow and wide boards are cut alternately from a quarter section of a log. This gets the most usable and the strongest boards from the section of the log.

Rottenstone A fine powder abrasive made from crushing decomposed limestone. Rottenstone and oil are used as a fine finishing polish.

Rubbing varnish A finish material designed to provide an unusually high gloss when polished with rottenstone and oil.

Sanding block A padded wood block around which a piece of sandpaper is wrapped for hand sanding of a surface.

Sanding sealer A thinned shellac or other lightweight clear finish applied to wood to prevent the raising of wood grain by stain, filler or final finish material.

Sandpaper A coated abrasive—usually flint, garnet or aluminum oxide glued to a paper, cloth or plastic backing. It is used for smoothing or polishing woods.

Sash weight A weight held by a cord or wire to a window sash section to balance the weight of the sash so the window may be opened or closed easily or left partially open at a desired level.

Shellac A final, clear finish material created by dissolving lac flakes in denatured alcohol. A five pound cut of shellac is made by dissolving five pounds of lac flakes in one gallon of denatured alcohol. A one pound cut is one pound of flakes in a gallon of alcohol.

Softwood Wood that comes from logs of conebearing (coniferous) trees.

Spanish windlass A clamping device made by twisting a length of rope around the object. The tension is held by a dowel inserted in the rope and braced against the clamped object.

Spline A thin piece of wood used as a wedge. In a worn joint, a spline may be inserted into a cut to enlarge a dowel or a tenon so that the section will fit more tightly into the joint hole or mortise.

Spokeshave A tool designed to shape spokes or spindles when they cannot be shaped by turning on a lathe.

Stain Any of various forms of water, latex or oil based transparent or opaque coloring agents designed to penetrate the surface of

the wood to color (stain) the material.

Stenciling Transfering a pattern by applying paint, usually a special lacquer base paint, to a surface through the cut out areas of a stencil mask.

Stop molding A flat lath or grooved wood piece nailed to a window or door frame to limit the degree of swing or movement of the door or window sash.

Subfloor Plywood or planking laid directly over the joists to support final finish flooring.

Tack rag A piece of cheesecloth or other lint-free fabric treated with turpentine and a small amount of varnish to create a sticky or tacky quality so the rag will pick up and hold all dirt, dust and lint that it touches.

Tooth A slight roughness created by light sanding of a smooth surface. The tooth allows a new application of a high gloss finish to adhere to a previously laid down high gloss finish.

Toxic Poisonous

Trompe l'oeil A phrase meaning fool the eye used to describe painting that is so realistic that it appears to have three dimensions.

Tung oil A water resistant finishing oil/varnish ingredient made from crushed tung tree seeds. Tung oil dries more quickly than linseed oil.

Varnish A durable clear finish made of a mixture of resins, oil and alcohol or other volatile spirits. Varnish dries to a hard, smooth surface.

Veneer A thin sheet of wood applied to another piece of wood. Fine wood veneer is used in furniture.

Veneer tape A length of narrow veneer wood that can be glued to an edge of a table or cabinet shelf to hide plywood layers or to match other veneered surfaces.

Wet into wet Application of paint, clear finishes or stains so that fresh brush loads of material overlap the last area of application. This allows the line between strokes to be smoothed over showing no demarcations on the surface.

Wood filler Liquid, paste, putty or plaster materials designed to fill in holes or grain lines so that final finishes may be applied to a smooth surface.

Index

Contributors, picture credits

We wish to extend our thanks to the individuals, associations and manufacturers who graciously provided information and photographs for this book, and to Wolfgang Thoma, Fritz Koelbel, and Al Dawson who provided guidance during the initial development of the manuscript. Specific credit for individual photographs is given below.

Capital letters following page numbers indicate: T, *top;* B, *bottom;* L, *left;* R, *right;* C, *center*

Almilmo Corporation c/o Hayes-Williams, Incorporated 261 Madison Ave., New York, NY 10016 *(p. 125 UL, 131 T)* **American Olean Tile,** 2583 Cannon Ave., Lansdale, PA 19446 *(p. 71 U)* **American Plywood Association,** Box 1119A, Tacoma, WA 98401 *(p. 33 LL, 34 C and LR)* **Architectural Woodwork Co.,** Carl Bullmore, 1715 20th St., Racine, WI 53403 **Armstrong Cork Company,** Liberty Street, Lancaster, PA 17604 *(p. 104 R)*

Bendix Molding Inc., 235 Pegasus, Northwall, NJ 07647 *(p. 125 R)* **Bix Manufacturing Company, Inc.,** 1116 Fowler St., Old Hickory, TN 37138 *(p. 5, 15 LC, 29, 39 UL, R, 68)* **Jim Blankets,** 240 South Canon, Beverly Hills, CA 90212 *(p. 66, 67 U)* **Borden Chemical,** Consumer Products Div. 180 East Broad St., Columbus, Ohio 43215 **Bruce Hardwood Floors,** 4255 LBJ Freeway, Dallas, TX 75234 *(p. 8, 65, 95 U)* **Craig Buchanan,** photographer, 490 2nd St., San Francisco, CA 94107 *(p. 12)*

Albert Constantine and Son, Inc., 2050 Eastchester Road, New York, NY 10461

Devcon Company, Endicott Street, Danvers, MA 01923 **Tia Doyle,** photographer, 632 West Deming, Chicago, IL 60614 *(p. 96 UR, L, 98 UR, 100 LR, 102, 103)* **Drexel-Heritage Furnishings,** Drexel, NC 28619 *(p. 10 UL, 77 U)* **Margery Duke Antiques,** 341 North Milwaukee St., Milwaukee, WI 53202 *(p. 61 LR)*

Easy Time Wood Refinishing Products Corp., P.O. Box 686, Glen Ellyn, IL 60137

(p. 35 LL, C) **Ego Productions,** Charles W. Auer, M.M. Auer, 1849 N. 72nd St., Wauwatosa, WI 53213 *(p. 24 UR, L, RC, LL, 30 C, L, 31 UL, 37, 38 R, 42, 49 UL, 52 R, 55, 59, 60, 61 UL, 62, 64, 77 L, 84, 85, 86, 89, 88, 108, 109 UR, 126, 129, 131 L, 132 R, 133, 135, 136, 137)*

Georgia-Pacific Corp., 900 SW 5th St., Portland OR 97204 *(p. 6-7)*

Haas Cabinet Co., Inc., c/o Sumner Rider & Associates, 355 Lexington Ave., New York, NY 10017 *(p. 130)* **Len and Key Hilts,** 911 South Vine Streets, Hinsdale, IL 60521 *(32 UL, 41 L, C, 43, 134)* **Herb Hughes,** 3033 Willow La., Montgomery, AL 36109 *(p. 47 C, 69, 106 UL, 116 C, 118, 121 L)*

Janco Greenhouses, J.A. Nearing Co., Inc., 9390 Davis Ave., Laurel, MD 20810 *(p. 113 LR)* **S.C. Johnson & Son, Inc.,** Racine, Wisconsin 53403 J.T. Benson, Product Evaluation Section Manager *(p. 45, 46 UR, 100 L)*

Joseph Kaminsky, designer, 250 West 99th St., New York, NY 10025 *(p. 14)* **Lis King Public Relations,** Box 503, Mahwah, NJ 07430 *(p. 67 LL, 72, 74, 75, 76 L, 105 L, 109 LR)* **Kleanstrip,** P.O. Box 1879, Memphis, TN 38101

Law J. Litzau, architectural, interior and graphic designer, 225 East St. Paul, Milwaukee, WI 53202 *(p. 93, 117 L, 124)* **Louisiana Pacific Corp.,** Portland, Oregon *(p. 107)*

Mary McLaughlin, managing editor, *Working Mother Magazine, (p. 9)* **Majestic Fireplaces,** 8150 Zionsville Rd., Indianapolis, IN 46268 *(p. 117 U)* **Marvin Windows,** Warroad, MN 56163 *(p. 106, 107 C)* **Minwax Company,** c/o Gilbert, Whitney & Johns, Inc., 44 Dumont Place, Morristown, NJ 07960 *(p. 49 LC, 50 LL, 51 L, 68 MR, 119 U, 120 U)* **Benjamin Moore and Company,** Chestnut Ridge Road, Montvale, NJ 07645 *(p. 40 UL, 52 L, 53 R, 54 L, 97 UR, 98 LR, 99, 101, 120 LL, 121 UR, 127 UR)* **David Morgan,** 129 West 76th Street, New York, NY 10023 *(p. 14 UR)*

National Paint & Coatings, *(p. 70, 74 R)* **Richard V. Nunn,** Media Mark Productions, Falls Church Inn, 6633 Arlington Blvd. Falls Church, VA 22045 *(p. 16, 19 UR, 56, 94 RC, L, 95 L, 106 LL, C, 112 LC, 113 C, LL, 119 L, 122, 123 UR, 138 L)*

Tom Philbin, 14 Lakeside Drive, Centerport, NY 11721 *(p. 17, 19 L, 20 U, LR, 21, 22, 24 LR, 25, 27, 30 UC, 35 R, 38 L, 39 L, 40 LR, 41 R, 46 L, 47 L, 50 UL, C, LR, 51 C, R, 57, 76 R, 81, 82, 83, 90 U, 94 CU, L, 96 L, 97 UL, 110, 111, 112 UC, R, 113 U, 114, 115, 123 UL, 127 LL, 128, 132)* **Pittsburgh Paint and Glass,** One Gateway Center, Pittsburgh, PA 15222 *(p. 44, 54 R, 61 UR, 78-79, 91 L, 120 LC)*

Ready-Built Products, P.O. Box 4306, Baltimore, MD 21223, *(p. 47 LR)* **Red Devil Paints & Chemicals,** 30 North West Street, Mount Vernon, NY 10550 **Rustic Crafts,** 65 West Sheffield Ave., Englewood, NJ 07631 *(p. 49)*

The Savogran Company, 259 Lenox Street, (P.O. Box 130) Norwood, MA 02062 **Scranton Photo Studio,** 322 N. Washington Ave., Scranton, PA 18503 *(p. 92, 104 L)* **Sears, Roebuck and Co.,** Sears Tower-233 South Wacker, Chicago, IL. 60606 **Thomas Strahan,** c/o Lis King Public Relations, Box 503, Mahwah, NJ 07430 *(p. 67 LR)* **Styletex,** c/o Lis King-Public Relations, Box 503, Mahwah, NJ 07430 *(p. 71 L)*

The 3M Company, 3M Center, 223-IN, St. Paul, MN 55144 *(p. 20 LL, 73 LC, L)*

United Gilsonite Laboratories, P.O. Box 70, Scranton, PA 18501 *(p. 11, 40L, 68 LR)*

Vikwood Ltd., Robert Larson, Box 554 (1221A Superior), Sheboygan, WI 53081 (fine, rare woods and veneers)

James Eaton Weeks, Interior Designs, Inc., 223 East Silver Spring Drive, Milwaukee, WI 53217 *(p. 127 LR)* **Western Wood Products Association,** Yeon Building, Portland, OR 97204 *(p. 109 LL)* **Wood Moulding & Millwork Producers,** P.O. Box 25278, Portland, OR 97225

LUMBER

Sizes: Metric cross-sections are so close to their nearest Imperial sizes, as noted below, that for most purposes they may be considered equivalents.

Lengths: Metric lengths are based on a 300mm module which is slightly shorter in length than an Imperial foot. It will therefore be important to check your requirements accurately to the nearest inch and consult the table below to find the metric length required.

Areas: The metric area is a square metre. Use the following conversion factors when converting from Imperial data: 100 sq. feet = 9.290 sq. metres.

METRIC SIZES SHOWN BESIDE NEAREST IMPERIAL EQUIVALENT

mm	Inches	mm	Inches
16 x 75	⅝ x 3	44 x 150	1¾ x 6
16 x 100	⅝ x 4	44 x 175	1¾ x 7
16 x 125	⅝ x 5	44 x 200	1¾ x 8
16 x 150	⅝ x 6	44 x 225	1¾ x 9
19 x 75	¾ x 3	44 x 250	1¾ x 10
19 x 100	¾ x 4	44 x 300	1¾ x 12
19 x 125	¾ x 5	50 x 75	2 x 3
19 x 150	¾ x 6	50 x 100	2 x 4
22 x 75	⅞ x 3	50 x 125	2 x 5
22 x 100	⅞ x 4	50 x 150	2 x 6
22 x 125	⅞ x 5	50 x 175	2 x 7
22 x 150	⅞ x 6	50 x 200	2 x 8
25 x 75	1 x 3	50 x 225	2 x 9
25 x 100	1 x 4	50 x 250	2 x 10
25 x 125	1 x 5	50 x 300	2 x 12
25 x 150	1 x 6	63 x 100	2½ x 4
25 x 175	1 x 7	63 x 125	2½ x 5
25 x 200	1 x 8	63 x 150	2½ x 6
25 x 225	1 x 9	63 x 175	2½ x 7
25 x 250	1 x 10	63 x 200	2½ x 8
25 x 300	1 x 12	63 x 225	2½ x 9
32 x 75	1¼ x 3	75 x 100	3 x 4
32 x 100	1¼ x 4	75 x 125	3 x 5
32 x 125	1¼ x 5	75 x 150	3 x 6
32 x 150	1¼ x 6	75 x 175	3 x 7
32 x 175	1¼ x 7	75 x 200	3 x 8
32 x 200	1¼ x 8	75 x 225	3 x 9
32 x 225	1¼ x 9	75 x 250	3 x 10
32 x 250	1¼ x 10	75 x 300	3 x 12
32 x 300	1¼ x 12	100 x 100	4 x 4
38 x 75	1½ x 3	100 x 150	4 x 6
38 x 100	1½ x 4	100 x 200	4 x 8
38 x 125	1½ x 5	100 x 250	4 x 10
38 x 150	1½ x 6	100 x 300	4 x 12
38 x 175	1½ x 7	150 x 150	6 x 6
38 x 200	1½ x 8	150 x 200	6 x 8
38 x 225	1½ x 9	150 x 300	6 x 12
44 x 75	1¾ x 3	200 x 200	8 x 8
44 x 100	1¾ x 4	250 x 250	10 x 10
44 x 125	1¾ x 5	300 x 300	12 x 12

METRIC LENGTHS

Lengths Metres	Equiv. Ft. & Inches
1.8m	5' 10⅞"
2.1m	6' 10⅝"
2.4m	7' 10½"
2.7m	8' 10¼"
3.0m	9' 10⅛"
3.3m	10' 9⅞"
3.6m	11' 9¾"
3.9m	12' 9½"
4.2m	13' 9⅜"
4.5m	14' 9⅓"
4.8m	15' 9"
5.1m	16' 8¾"
5.4m	17' 8⅝"
5.7m	18' 8⅜"
6.0m	19' 8¼"
6.3m	20' 8"
6.6m	21' 7⅞"
6.9m	22' 7⅝"
7.2m	23' 7½"
7.5m	24' 7¼"
7.8m	25' 7⅛"

All the dimensions are based on 1 inch = 25 mm.

NOMINAL SIZE (This is what you order.)	ACTUAL SIZE (This is what you get.)
Inches	**Inches**
1 x 1	¾ x ¾
1 x 2	¾ x 1½
1 x 3	¾ x 2½
1 x 4	¾ x 3½
1 x 6	¾ x 5½
1 x 8	¾ x 7¼
1 x 10	¾ x 9¼
1 x 12	¾ x 11¼
2 x 2	1¾ x 1¾
2 x 3	1½ x 2½
2 x 4	1½ x 3½
2 x 6	1½ x 5½
2 x 8	1½ x 7¼
2 x 10	1½ x 9¼
2 x 12	1½ x 11¼

WOOD SCREWS

SCREW GAUGE NO.	NOMINAL DIAMETER Inch	mm	LENGTH Inch	mm
0	0.060	1.52	³/₁₆	4.8
1	0.070	1.78	¼	6.4
2	0.082	2.08	⁵/₁₆	7.9
3	0.094	2.39	⅜	9.5
4	0.0108	2.74	⁷/₁₆	11.1
5	0.122	3.10	½	12.7
6	0.136	3.45	⅝	15.9
7	0.150	3.81	¾	19.1
8	0.164	4.17	⅞	22.2
9	0.178	4.52	1	25.4
10	0.192	4.88	1¼	31.8
12	0.220	5.59	1½	38.1
14	0.248	6.30	1¾	44.5
16	0.276	7.01	2	50.8
18	0.304	7.72	2¼	57.2
20	0.332	8.43	2½	63.5
24	0.388	9.86	2¾	69.9
28	0.444	11.28	3	76.2
32	0.5	12.7	3¼	82.6
			3½	88.9
			4	101.6
			4½	114.3
			5	127.0
			6	152.4

Dimensions taken from BS1210; metric conversions are approximate.

BRICKS AND BLOCKS

Bricks

Standard metric brick measures 215 mm x 65 mm x 112.5. Metric brick can be used with older, standard brick by increasing the mortaring in the joints. The sizes are substantially the same, the metric brick being slightly smaller (3.6 mm less in length, 1.8 mm in width, and 1.2 mm in depth).

Concrete Block

Standard sizes

390 x 90 mm
390 x 190 mm
440 x 190 mm
440 x 215 mm
440 x 290 mm

Repair block for replacement of block in old installations is available in these sizes:
448 x 219 (including mortar joints)
397 x 194 (including mortar joints)

NAILS

NUMBER PER POUND OR KILO

Size	Weight Unit	Common	Casing	Box	Finishing
2d	Pound	876	1010	1010	1351
	Kilo	1927	2222	2222	2972
3d	Pound	586	635	635	807
	Kilo	1289	1397	1397	1775
4d	Pound	316	473	473	548
	Kilo	695	1041	1041	1206
5d	Pound	271	406	406	500
	Kilo	596	893	893	1100
6d	Pound	181	236	236	309
	Kilo	398	591	519	680
7d	Pound	161	210	210	238
	Kilo	354	462	462	524
8d	Pound	106	145	145	189
	Kilo	233	319	319	416
9d	Pound	96	132	132	172
	Kilo	211	290	290	398
10d	Pound	69	94	94	121
	Kilo	152	207	207	266
12d	Pound	64	88	88	113
	Kilo	141	194	194	249
16d	Pound	49	71	71	90
	Kilo	108	156	156	198
20d	Pound	31	52	52	62
	Kilo	68	114	114	136
30d	Pound	24	46	46	
	Kilo	53	101	101	
40d	Pound	18	35	35	
	Kilo	37	77	77	
50d	Pound	14			
	Kilo	31			
60d	Pound	11			
	Kilo	24			

LENGTH AND DIAMETER IN INCHES AND CENTIMETERS

Size	Length Inches	Centimeters	Diameter Inches	Centimeters*
2d	1	2.5	068	17
3d	1·2	3.2	102	26
4d	1·4	3.8	102	26
5d	1·6	4.4	102	26
6d	2	5.1	115	29
7d	2·2	5.7	115	29
8d	2·4	6.4	131	33
9d	2·6	7.0	131	33
10d	3	7·6	148	38
12d	3·2	8.3	148	38
16d	3·4	8.9	148	38
20d	4	10·2	203	51
30d	4·4	11·4	220	58
40d	5	12.7	238	60
50d	5·4	14·0	257	66
60d	6	15.2	277	70

*Exact conversion

PIPE FITTINGS

Only fittings for use with copper pipe are affected by metrication: metric compression fittings are interchangeable with Imperial in some sizes, but require adaptors in others

INTERCHANGEABLE SIZES mm	Inches	SIZES REQUIRING ADAPTORS mm	Inches
12	⅜	22	¾
15	½	35	1¼
28	1	42	1½
54	2		

Metric capillary (soldered) fittings are not directly interchangeable with imperial sizes but adaptors are available. Pipe fittings which use screwed threads to make the joint remain unchanged. The British Standard Pipe (BSP) thread form has now been accepted internationally and its dimensions will not physically change. These screwed fittings are commonly used for joining iron or steel pipes, for connections on taps, basin and bath waste outlets and on boilers, radiators, pumps etc. Fittings for use with lead pipe are joined by soldering and for this purpose the metric and inch sizes are interchangeable.

(Information courtesy Metrication Board, Millbank Tower, Millbank, London SW1P 4QU)